"...it is in everyone and as we let our own light shine, we unconsciously give others permission to do the same. As we are liberated from our own fear, our presence automatically liberates others."

Marianne Williamson

Praise for the HeART of STORY

"I've been a storyteller for more than 30 years. But this wonderful book taught me many things I didn't know. Thank you Raju Mandhyan!"

—Bo Sanchez, bestselling author

"Raju Mandhyan has done a fantastic job of bringing to our consciousness the what, why, and how of corporate storytelling. Stories are realities wrapped in roses, rainbows, and rhythm. This is, after all, what a company needs to sell, to build its brand, to communicate with stakeholders, and to drive creativity and innovation. The HeART of STORY is beautifully written and is such a smooth read."

—Ashok Nath, Chairman, Exedra Events

"With 'The HeART of STORY' Raju Mandhyan, coach and corporate trainer, has effectively shown how an ancient art form and communication medium can be employed to facilitate human resource development in the modern world. This is a definitive book on this art. As one who comes from a society steeped in oral traditions and where stories played the main role in the transmission of our history, I greatly appreciate this endeavor of the author."

—Dunstan Chan, Speaker, Writer and Storyteller

"So we fix our eyes not on what is seen but on what is unseen. For what is unseen is eternal. This is the 'great value' of storytelling. It is passed on to be remembered. A long time ago I met this great prince named Raju Mandhyan. He has many great stories but more importantly he has a great heart. Since that day, we have lived happily as friends. Be inspired and learn from the wisdom of 'The HeART of STORY.'"

— Dean Pax Lapid, Dean of Entrepreneurship, Truly Rich Club and Chairman, IT-SPAC.

"The HeART of STORY is full of stories that convince the reader to put sizzle in the message so the audience is convinced, understands, and acts upon the truth. Each chapter makes a point backed by a story. Raju Mandhyan provides tools, examples from personal experiences, from business practices, and from leaders on the ground. We highly recommend this book to preachers, academicians, theologians, and all communicators of truth and faith who desire to capture the imagination and heart of their audience."

— Dr. Stewart and Dr. Corrie De Boer, Asian Theological Seminary, Philippines

Raju Mandhyan's The HeART of STORY reveals and revels in the magic of the attraction that the human race has had with stories since time immemorial. Unlike any other book I've read on the topic, Raju takes the reader behind the curtains of science, art, creativity, and business to make a powerful case to use stories to influence our world. He doesn't just tell, he demonstrates his truth with memorable stories that will stick with the reader. This book should find an avid following with any person or organization that wants to make their brand unforgettable.

— Dilip R. Abayasekara, Ph.D., Accredited Speaker
Past President, Toastmasters International (2005-2006)
Author of The Path of the Genie:
Your Journey to Your Heart's Desire.

From the king of storytelling himself.... now you can learn the secrets that will take you far in leadership and in life!

Scott Friedman,
National Speaker Association President 2004-2005
Certified Speaking Professional
2013 Winner of NSA Cavett Award
MPI Rise Award, CSP Global

THE HEART OF THE STORY

CONNECT, ENGAGE AND INFLUENCE YOUR AUDIENCE CREATIVELY

RAJU MANDHYAN

Foreword by:
Dr. Roland Sullivan

EBD
EMBASSY BOOKS
www.embassybooks.in

This edition first published in 2017

Published in India by:
Embassy Books
120, Great Western Building,
Maharashtra Chamber of Commerce Lane,
Fort, Mumbai - 400 023.
Tel : (91-22) 22819546 / 22818567.
Email : info@embassybooks.in
Website : www.embassybooks.in

Distribution Centres:
Mumbai, Ahmedabad, Bangalore, Kolkata, Chennai,
Hyderabad, New Delhi, Pune

ISBN: 978-93-86450-14-2

Foreword

After several years of working at cleansing and strengthening my mind, body and spirit one meditative moment an indescribable, internal, mysterious joy began to rise from my being still and quiet. It is then I reached out to my mentor Sri Nerode of India and asked if I could go see him.

I was at Sri Nerodes' side when he turned 90 and made a statement that, till today, rings like church bells in my mind and has become a living, dynamic story of my life. He claimed that he had changed and transformed into a much better human being in the last 90 days of his life than he had in all the past 90 years. That bold, powerful and amazing statement has become the story that drives me, relentlessly, to help organizations seek change, innovate and transform holistically regardless of their age, their structures or their resources.

At about the same period in my life, I was also being mentored by Dr. Warren Bennis, American Scholar, and organizational consultant and widely regarded as the pioneer of the contemporary field of leadership studies. His major theme, over the years, was that leadership starts with self-discovery, heightened awareness and mastering the art of sharing and eliciting heartfelt, transformative stories was the key and the path to extraordinary leadership. Dr. Warren Bennis also claimed that we will experience more change and transformation in our lives than that has been seen in the last 4500 years of recorded history of civilization. My trust is that will happen because of the stories that we plant, nourish and harvest.

Now, I am not an electrifying storyteller as Raju Mandhyan but the wisdom, the principles and the practices proposed in this book will be my guide and my reference for the work I do because I know that storytelling, especially of the positive and appreciative nature as cited in this book will be an element that will create the phenomenal change that Dr. Warren Bennis spoke about.

To the reader, I urge, take the contents of this seriously, combine them with a spirit of self-discovery, awareness and contemplation as you commit to changing your own life and helping others transform through the HeART of STORY.

Dr. Roland Sullivan
Original 100 Change Agent

Dedication

This book is dedicated to my daughter, Karishma, who, as a toddler, demanded I always come up with a new story at every bedtime — stories not read from books but hatched on the spot out of thin, thin air. Plus these stories, they had to make sense, entertain, and inspire her to float into her chosen dreamland every night.

Acknowledgement

Yes, it did all begin with tucking my kids into bed but somehow, somewhere, the child in me began to enjoy those moments. In fact, the addiction got so bad I would stop people in the stairways, in the elevators, and on the streets to let them have what was brewing inside my mind and heart.

Much, much later the world of Toastmasters let me into their circle and tamed my passion and gave it some form and purpose. The fun continued until I began to coach businesses and organizations into growth and improved results. That was when the amazing power behind stories and storytelling began to shape up my world.

I was being moved by stories of success and leadership I'd hear. I was able to inspire and motivate people by telling stories of excellence and successful practices by others. I was awed by how people embraced change when they could see their future in the form of narrative and storytelling. For this I thank the world of Appreciative Inquiry facilitators and consultants led by Dr. David Cooperrider in the USA and Dr. Rose Fuentes in the Philippines.

Inside

I

Once Upon a Time

Hundreds of years ago in a beautiful little village among the misty mountains of a land far, far way the clouds hung low, the birds flew high and the water from the brooks sang lullabies to the children at night.

This picture book pretty, little village was also famous for being home to two very beautiful women. These two beauties were the toast of the town and everyone loved them to bits. They were loved for how beautiful they were to look at; how nicely they moved and talked and sang and danced; and how, just by being beautiful as they were, they inspired all the people of that little village up in the misty mountains.

Alas, time passed, seasons changed, and the world spun around many a year; and these two beautiful women began to age. And, as it is often true with aging, these two beauties began to look less and less attractive to the people of that beautiful town nestled in the misty mountains.

One day, they eventually got tired and frustrated over getting less and less attention from the people of the town. They were tired of the fact that they hadn't hit the headlines of any newspapers or magazines in a long while and they were frustrated because their posts on Social Media Channels were getting no attention. They decided to take some serious action about the plunge in their popularity and about the change in how the people of that little village regarded and appreciated them. It was time to set things right.

So one evening, after a good day's rest and after doing all the little things beautiful women do to make themselves look lovelier, they chose to take a stroll down the town's Main Street dressed in their loveliest. Upon reaching the upper end of Main Street, said the First Beauty to the Second Beauty, "Allow me please, first, to walk down the street and see how the people appreciate and cheer me. Okay?"

With her chin held high she sweetly sashayed down Main Street expecting to get smiles, nods and waves from the village. Nothing happened. Not a single person glanced at her, nobody nodded, and no one smiled or waved at the First Beauty. This made her very, very sad.

"I want to try that again!" she wailed and she shook off the stole that wrapped her shoulders and ripped off the hem from her long skirt exposing her elegant shins. Boldly then, she marched back onto Main Street, sure that her exposed shoulders and shins were bound to attract attention in that sleepy old village up in the misty mountains. Again, nothing happened! No one noticed her. In fact, some elderly ladies who happened to glance at her twitched their noses in distaste. Men looked right through her and the children on the street just snuggled into their mothers' arms. She was heartbroken and devastated by this turnout.

This time, the third time, she became really angry and decided to get a lot bolder. With a lot of vengeance on her mind and very little clothing on her body, she stomped down Main Street in the little village. This time people turned their faces away in disgust. Mothers covered the eyes of their young ones and businessmen shut the doors and windows of their shops. There was no describing the horror and sadness that engulfed the First Beauty. She covered her face with her hands and began to sob vehemently.

Knowing it was her turn; the Second Beauty tightened the straps on her leather shoes and wrapped anklets with little bells on her shins. She also tightened the colorful, velveteen belt around her waistline, fluffed up the stole around her shoulders, added a few flowers into her hair, and let her bangles jangle. With huge smile lighting up her beautiful face, she hummingly' eased onto Main Street.

Lo and behold! On Main Street the women smiled and nodded at her; the men took a second look, some even taking off their hats to bow down low for her; and the little children snatched their hands away from their mothers' hands and ran to the Second beauty calling her "Bellissimo, bellissimo, bellissimo!" A strange, flowery aroma began to ascend from the earth in the little village; butterflies appeared from nowhere; and from somewhere far away, someone began to play the violin gently and to sweetly sing songs of praise for the Second Beauty.

Perhaps at about this time, you, dear reader, are wondering why these two beauties are being referred to as the First and the Second. Do they not have names, you ask?

Yes, that is a good question to ask and I'd like to give you time to ponder about that but this being a story in a book you hold in your hand, I cannot do that. So just sit back, take a deep breath and I shall give you the answer.

The name of the First Beauty is **Truth** and the name of the Second Beauty is **Story**.

The reality today is very few people in the world want to see or hear the bold truth. In fact, the bolder and starker the truth gets, the lesser attention it receives. It can, more often than not, be despised such that people thwart and rebel against it. And yet, the same beautiful truth when wrapped in color, garnished with flowers, and accompanied by song can become a reigning reality. That is the power of **Story.** Stories are core **Truths** wrapped in roses, rainbows and rhythm. That is the story behind storytelling.

History of Stories

Eons ago, when man discovered fire, he also discovered the wonder of telling stories around that fire. After a hard day's hunt, he would gather his tribe and begin to converse and tell great stories. He told stories about the source of life, about the sun, about the moon and the stars. He also told stories about the time and place where the sun was born and how the moon romanced it. He told stories about how the moon pursued the sun and died every month to be reborn to love the sun all over again. He told stories about how every individual had a star of his own up in the teal and midnight-blue skies.

Day after day, night upon night, from one season to another, man told stories –tales about love, courage, adventure, conquest, and wars. Around the fire, he told stories of ferocious Spartan warriors and heroes that battled one-eyed giants. He told stories about birds that could fly into the sun, burst into cinder, and then rise again from the ashes to fly right back into the sun.

Over the ages, stories of tradition, honor, and great courage ruled the air around the fires. There were stories told about great escapes, bold robberies, and giant shipwrecks.

Discoveries were reported about new worlds, new wealth, and new people. Narrated with rhyme, repetition, and rhythm, all these stories were etched on the walls of the caves where our ancestors lived and into the hearts and minds of all mankind. Shadows and echoes from the flickering fires left unforgettable legends visualized and represented on the walls of our current homes. Today, many of these stories have become a large part of belief systems, of our culture and our tradition.

Science behind Stories

What exactly is the science behind a story? Why do stories stir up so much of our emotions and our humanity? Why do they have such a lasting effect on us? What happens when we tell stories? What happens to people when they listen to a story? What happens to me when I tell a story?

Firstly, as I tell the story, I begin to relive the experience. I relive the wonder and the excitement that is part of the truth in the story. As I use my left brain to recreate the setting, the context, and the characters involved, my right brain jumps in to participate by offering images, colors, sounds, and textures. Then, both my left and the right brain begin to have fun together and go to play. The whole exercise of storytelling becomes a whole brain activity for me, the storyteller.

The second amazing secret behind this whole activity where the brain goes to play is the fact that this sense of play is also very contagious. How is it contagious? It releases endorphins and other sweet smells of bliss and fun that draw in and attract other people to join. Because this activity was started by the left brain setting up a logical scene and then was ignited by the right brain firing up a party, the minds of all those around fully participate in the thrill by suspending their wariness and dropping their normal cerebral resistance to novelty. This phenomenon is quite similar to when we see people dance and we are drawn in to join the dance.

When we see a bunch of people on the street joyfully laughing and playing, our own spirits light up. If inhibitions are holding us back, we feel like dropping them and jumping right into the fun. In storytelling, the listeners' minds begin to likewise log in, plug in, and salsa with our imagination and train of thoughts. They do this regardless of how much or how little they know about the story background or about the storyteller's experience. This is because as we create and put up verbal holograms/holographs in the conversation space, the listeners also set up movie screens in their minds and watch movies of their own making, with themselves as the main character. The movie we are putting across through storytelling inspires and projects a parallel movie in their minds. The images, colors, sounds, and drama in our conversations spark multiple, similar, copies of scenes running in the minds of our audience. This is magic in action.

This is exactly why the streets of Hollywood glitter with gold. Because in our minds and in the minds of countless audiences, we all think and believe we are part of the magic and mystique that rises out of Hollywood. In my mind, I am Peter Pan or the Lone Ranger and you must be Dr. Livingstone, I presume?

This is synergy and co-creativity in action. This is the real story behind the power of storytelling.

Now, the third most powerful thing about stories and storytelling is the fact that they impact the deepest part of our brain and our emotions. They cut through our cerebral defenses and sink in. What are cerebral defenses and why do they have to be surpassed? The human brain of a newborn baby comes with some pre-embedded coding towards his traits and character. These are acquired from parental traits and characters. This is genetics. Right after birth, the newborn baby's brain starts to absorb and accumulate data from what he sees, hears, smells, touches, and tastes. This data gathers fast, accumulates rapidly, and integrates really swiftly in early childhood. All this data is acquired and stored in the form of pixels, sound bytes, touch and other modalities of sensory inputs.

Most of the data that is primarily absorbed, accumulated, and integrated acquires importance over time. They maintain their importance throughout our lives. We call them our values and beliefs. We can be, and we do turn emotional about our values and beliefs. Emotions burst out from thinking of things sensitive to us—images, sounds and

when you start telling a story, it helps others recall and relive their own stories, their own experiences.

smells that have been around us, within us for a long time. Our emotions, thus, are the stories of our lives.

All forms of communication address and tap into recent memories that are not ancient or primal to us. Storytelling is the exception. All other forms of communication connect with images, ounds, and smells acquired not so long ago that reside in our recent memories. This neighborhood of our "recent" memories is a highly congested, constantly active desktop of chaos and novelty. And the older and tender memories of our growing years fear and avoid such chaos and congestion.

When narrating and listening to stories, the sights, sounds, aromas, textures, and flavors from our growing-up, formative years begin to surface.

They burst through the fear of the current, cerebral chaos and part through it like an old, bearded man once mythically parted the sea to get his people across to the other side.

Every time we tune into a story, the chaos and the confusion of cognition fall away to make a path so our emotions easily dance with the emotions expressed by the storyteller, as we see and hear them. Every time our emotions are happily touched, we become eager to do something, to take action, to build new things, and to stretch our limits as individuals, communities, and organizations.

Storytelling Today

The ancient art of storytelling has turned into a science riding on the wave of television and technology as a laughing, talking, singing universe. This universe now surrounds us twenty-four hours a day and also reaches us through books, song, dance, stage-plays, movies, television, computers, and phones. It does not let go even when we are 10 kilometers up in the air and zooming across the skies at over 500 kilometers per hour. Stories grab us in news reports, magazine shows, commercials, documentaries, television serials, musicals, and films of epic proportions. Stories reach us through multiple media in formats like short episodes, interactive applications, gaming applications, etc.

The ancient, traditional face-to-face, oral storytelling has also morphed with the integration of poetry, improvisation, mime, and other forms. Seasoned, professional storytellers can keep us awe-struck and engaged in their verbal and non-verbal gymnastics for hours on end. Seasoned storytellers, thus, can influence and positively transform our worlds.

2

Stories, How they Serve Organizations

Today, there are huge developmental benefits that stories and storytelling deliver beyond unleashing creativity, using metaphors, and the philosophy that backs them. Yes, stories in storytelling are not just about people. They are also about nurturing the planet and pushing up the profits in business.

Stories help us connect with distant entities and cultures. Stories sustain and consistently enhance the levels of engagement within our own organizations, communities and cultures. Stories are the magical and metaphorical processes by which we can ethically influence our market and all our stakeholders in a creative manner.

Stories Strengthen your Brand and Identity

Coca- Cola in the US, Tata Motors in India, and Jollibee in the Philippines are not just names and good products. They also have a very specific character and a whole personality attached to their names.

Utter the name of Coca-Cola and suddenly, the cognitive and perceptual screen in consumers' minds explode with brilliant fireworks. Phrases like "It's the Real Thing, Coke Adds Life, Coke is it!" constantly pop into our heads. Beyond the immediate responses related to its, name there is also the assurance of quality, performance, and a unique dependability in all Coca-Cola products. This type of response and relationship with the consumer did not come about just recently. It came from an accumulation of thousands of experiences, emotions, and stories attached to the product and its partnership with people.

Coca-Cola is aware of this so it nurtures and protects this massive, intangible asset with the same ferociousness it applies in guarding its secret formula for producing the bubbly, cola drink. Coca-Cola knows this so it regularly fuels the fires that keep this relationship burning by creating new stories, new emotional attachments with its customers.

A few years ago, Coca- Cola churned up heart-warming emotions between India and Pakistan by putting up vending machines using 3D touch screen technology so that the peoples of these quarreling nations were able to see and mime and touch each other, virtually.

The history and relationship of these culturally similar countries and people is that from being one country, it was split in two more than sixty years ago. Many factions on both sides are still upset over the split that happened in 1947. Each side is still unhappy about friends, memories, and homes that they left behind during what was called the "partition." They have fought several wars since then, quarreled over borders in the beautiful state of Kashmir, and blamed each other for cheating in sporting events. Generally, their people are extremely suspicious of one other. It was a gargantuan task for Coca-cola to bring together these two peoples into a life-sized, virtual interaction.

The campaign called *Small World Machines* provided a live communications portal linking strangers across the borders of India and Pakistan. First-of-its-kind 3D touchscreen technology projected a streaming video feed onto the vending machine screen while simultaneously filming through the unit to capture a live emotional exchange between people miles away from each other.

Jackie Jantos, former Global Creative Director of Coca-Cola, claimed that the idea of creating stories around shared experiences went back to its roots. Coke started at a soda fountain which in itself is a communal experience. The India-Pakistan interaction might have been a virtual one but the emotions were real and open-hearted. The project not only endeared the Coca-Cola brand but also earned a lot of respect for Coke.

Mention the name of Tata in India and every loyal Indian consumer will raise her chin higher as her eyes light up in approval. For nearly 75 years now, Tata and all its divisions have been serving the Indian nation well. Yes, they had a difficult start in the troubled times before Indian independence, but they persistently held on, determined to focus on quality and to serve a young and a hungry nation. Over the years, families, employees, and all other stakeholders in the Tata group of companies have each had a story of his own to tell. In the 1960s and 70s, skilled workers would queue up for jobs in the production lines of Tata Motors. Once in, they would consider themselves successfully settled and would stay with Tata for life. Such was, and still is, the reputation of Tata Group of Companies in India.

Tata knows this and consistently organizes and aligns itself to the image and expectations that stakeholders look for in this brand. In the 1990s when the Indian economy picked up momentum and produced a larger middle class, Tata realigned itself to the growing needs of a new nation by providing them with the world's cheapest and most fuel-efficient car, the Nano. Today, Tata continues to be ranked the number one brand in India and among the top 50 brand stories of the world. Images, emotions, and relationships in the form of stories have been the drivers behind this magnificent performance and brand from India.

In the Philippines, no matter how many times it is repeated, the story of how Jollibee Hamburgers started off as a little family-owned ice cream parlor always brings a sense of pride. This success story is wrapped in deep, powerful Filipino values of family cohesiveness, nationalism, and the endeavor to constantly improve and innovate. Embedded in this brand story is the legendary David-and-Goliath plot of how a small, insignificant entity took on a giant, global hamburger chain and brought it to its feet.

Regardless of another global brand's performance being a few notches higher in the world stage than that of Jollibee, its "story" as being born of a humble Filipino enterprise that respects and appreciates family and togetherness makes Jollibee the nation's best-seller. Jollibee knows this to be the reigning reality. They continuously exert all-out efforts to improve their products, service, and performance not just to elevate quality standards but also because they are motivated by the stories that come with the brand. They are smart to do so. It makes good business sense and it makes good developmental sense. Living up to your brand stories is a sensible and a strategic ideal.

Stories as Drivers of Engagement and Innovation

Stories may be truths wrapped in roses, rainbows, and rhythm, but they also create the future–that which is possible and which can indeed be beautiful.

When organizations slow down or arrive at a difficult bend in their developmental journey, people within the organization need hope. They need new dreams and fresh inspiration. Success stories from the past empower us, but it is the stories into the future–stories yet to be lived–that catapult us into action and success.

These words are etched on the mental corridors of workers in this company that supplies milk and milk derivatives to nearly half the world.

Individuals are shaped by different experiences yet our shared values enable us to combine our strengths to make us innovative and successful. There are just four simple truths that guide us: spirit of co-operation, doing what is right, challenging boundaries, and making it happen.

These values are images that are colorful and crystal-clear to the farmers and managers of Fonterra of New Zealand. The clarity and vividness make these values a dynamic living image. It is the vision and the story that serves as the springboard for creating an unfolding future, a future they continue to create.

Made up of over 400 members, this co-operative has been around for over a hundred years. They have been steadily growing for decades and have consistently and continuously become efficient and innovative. Why? Because where they have come from is clear in this organization, and where they are heading to, is just as crystal clear.

The vivid, colorful story of the future in their minds drives them to easily implement relevant changes every day. The living, dynamic, future-projected story is a compelling magnet. It becomes a self-driven desire to change rather than something that the organization members need to be cajoled and pushed into. Furthermore, this story of their future is easily communicated and has the potential of naturally turning viral in the organization.

A Story: Honoring Heritage

Telling stories that engage audiences across a campfire or through movies is one thing, but how do you make an organizational story flourish and honor the heritage of its founders? How do you take its core values, which were espoused and lived decades ago, and impress and impact modern-day realities of a 14,000-member-strong organization?

The answer is through the digital medium.

The Lopez Group of Companies in the Philippines was born in 1928 and was led in the early years by its founder Eugenio "Eñing" Lopez, Sr. In the ensuing years it was then led by Eñing's eldest son, Eugenio "Genny" Lopez, Jr followed by his younger brother, octogenarian, Oscar Lopez. The conglomerate is currently headed by Oscar's younger brother, Ambassador Manuel M. Lopez.

The Lopez Group has large interests in media, telecommunications, power generation, property and infrastructure development, and manufacturing, among others. The group is well respected, both locally and globally, for its sound, ethical management practices. It espouses and truly acts upon the set of values originally inspired by its founders. These values are rooted in integrity, nationalism, justice, unity, and the welfare of the 14,000 people who work for the group.

In recent years, the second generation members of the Lopez Family began taking over the management of its operations. These new leaders wanted to re-establish and reinforce those values to their newer recruits and members. The question was how to effectively reach out to a large mass of 14,000 people. Traditional methods of meetings, conferences, summits, etc. would be time consuming and expensive. The answer lay in telling stories of success and best practices through the digital medium.

At first there was trepidation over how to start, sustain, and succeed with such an important campaign through a medium that utilizes pixels and sound bytes. The medium–especially its social aspect–was fickle and uncontrollable. A controversial picture, a misconstrued word, a slip of the tongue could spread like wild fire and fly on the wings of a very active bird called Twitter.

Yet the times, they were a-changing and changing fast! Conglomerates around the world were hopping onto the bandwagon, and staying behind was not an option for the Lopez Group. They would have to ride the waves of change. The decision to digitally re-ignite the flames of their credo had to be taken.

On the 82nd anniversary of the Lopez Group, all the top managers and CEOs of their different subsidiaries as well as the heads of Communications and of Human Resources departments were brought together. The announcement was then issued and the project was launched.

Next, scores of focus group discussions and seminars were held that were a combination of values reinforcement and learning events. The outcome of each event was filled with stories of success that resulted from adhering to best practices in the decision making processes of the Lopez Group founders and leaders. The values of integrity, nationalism, justice, unity, and the welfare of the 14,000 people was a top topic, followed by the practice of leading by example and an inclusive management style.

These same top values and their applications were printed on wallet-sized cards and distributed across the organization. Such a traditional method was something the Lopez Group wanted to maintain, and it makes neurological sense to me. Images and words that you want to hold dear, want to remember always, and want to make a part of your psyche must be kept in close, physical and organic contact. It is a method of learning and memorizing that is reinforced through kinesthesia, through what is also known as muscle memory.

Following the card distribution, websites, blog-sites, and social media pages were all rehashed and updated. And then the Chairman Oscar Lopez began sending out direct, personal emails to just about everyone in the family that was the Lopez Group. The front-liners and newcomers to the group were ecstatic upon hearing directly from their leaders. One response read, "Your message inspires me, professionally and personally. It gives encouragement and makes me a better me every day."

When the elder Lopez shared the story of his climb of Mount Kinabalu, hundreds of members of the Lopez Group included that wish in their own bucket list. "This story of yours is inspiring and I cheer you on to the next mountain challenge. I was choosing between trying mountain climbing and planting more trees. Now I will look for friends who like mountain climbing. Sir, congratulations for conquering Mt. Kinabalu!"

When another senior Lopez Group leader sent a direct message to a media technician on a social site, the media technician who had been working with the group for 22 years was beyond joy to have been directly contacted by one of his icons. Any virtual or real-life observations of their leaders doing simple things in their lives became stories of great inspiration for their large followers.

To keep the online buzz and excitement alive, the Lopez Communications department launched essay contests, photo contests, and quizzes. Every action and project, each post, click, buzz, and share continued to strengthen their values and engagement across the whole organization. All these actions intensified and deepened their brand, their culture. Their leadership style came alive.

The Lopez Communications department has been very pleased with these outcomes. I would not be surprised if, one day, they take these interactions to the next level and launch applications and platforms where the group's leaders and the workers will be represented by animated versions and caricatures of themselves to interact with each other, comic-book style.

You could say that the old form of organizational storytelling is blazing through today's digital space at the speed of millions of megabits per second.

Stories as Strategies for Selling and Marketing

Ever since the first salesperson stood up on a soapbox and plugged away the scripted benefits of a heal-all, cure-all and save-all snake oil, people have become wary of commercials. They are tired of producers and salespersons pushing new products with added features in their faces. Commercials have not just invaded our homes through magazine, radio, and TV ads; they have also appeared on our dinner placemats, sports arenas, and our hand-held devices and phones. A former actor-comedian John Cleese, now a professor of creativity and marketing, claims marketing professionals are aware that 70-80% of their commercials and advertisements have no direct impact on sales. Yet, according to him, marketing and advertising professionals continue plaguing the world with commercials for the sake of keeping their industry alive.

The same is true about other forms of direct selling, whether to individual customers or large businesses. Salespeople keep on making linear, unidirectional, hackneyed presentations about how useful, and beneficial their products are without being concerned if all the noise they make with their flyer distributions, PowerPoint presentations, and product demonstrations make any impact at all. The truth is buyers do not buy when they are told to or sold to. They buy when their minds, memories, and emotions do a pivot upon hearing a story. It is a story that reaches out and touches them, and it is that story that engages them and turns their hearts around.

A very simple example might be that of a salesperson talking about how good the location, the construction, the price, and the potential appreciation of a piece of property is. The same salesperson becomes amazingly more effective when he explains how the former owner, Mrs. Anderson, personally supervised the construction of the place. He can follow with another story about how the present price– much lower than the current market value– helped Mr. Smith sell his property down the street with a whopping 25% gain within a year of having purchased it.

The whole tenet of wrapping real, valuable truth in the colorful images of a story promotes the truth easily and happily. The stories, of course, must be relevantly parallel and put across a simple, honest truth—buying the product makes good sense.

A Story: Soft Tough

Detox Chemicals of the Philippines produces and mixes industrial cleaners on demand that are tailor-fit solutions to their customers' specific needs. So if an engineering company needs a mixture that will remove clots of oxidation on underwater marine pipes they call upon Detox Chemicals. Detox Chemicals will run a few tests in their little laboratories and respond with solutions for them in less than a week. Their products rarely fail and because of this, Detox has gained great goodwill. Unfortunately, the goodwill generated was with agents, dealers, and other middlemen but not with the end customer. For years, scores of these middlemen acquired solutions from Detox and then glued a label of their own brand before sending them over to the end user.

A year ago Detox CEO, Alex Reyes wised up to the situation and decided to hit the marketplace himself to, hopefully, build a network of his own sales agents. He decided to create a singular, multi-purpose cleaning solution as their flagship product and hit the road selling it to retailers and end-users. The product that Detox mixed together was made of organic chemicals, had no side effects, was totally harmless to humans but served as a powerful answer to basic cleaning needs of various industries and even homes.

A few months after launching the flagship product called Soft Tough, he began calling upon retailers and other buyers, but Soft Tough failed to impress his prospective customers. Every time he walked into a potential client's office he would start talking about its efficacy, its biodegradable contents, its molecular mix, and how about how qualified a scientist he was. Day after day, week after week, the potential buyers remained unimpressed. Alex could not understand. He knew from experience the product was very safe and yet powerfully potent. He knew it was priced right and packaged correctly.

At home with his wife one day, he shared his concern and frustrations. His company had invested a huge amount of money in designing and packaging the product. Because they trusted their product they had also stored up a huge inventory. They needed to break the shackle-hold their previous dealers and agents had on them, but the investment was beginning to create cash flow issues. "I don't get it. The product is good and the pricing is right. We've done all the tests and have gotten FDA approval. The market needs it and we've made it such that even if it was consumed by humans it'd have no side effects!" he lamented. "Then why don't you tell your buyers this." suggested his wife. "What? Tell them Detox will go into the red if they don't buy from us?" "No, silly, tell them that it is powerful for cleaning and yet harmless to humans, just like you told me now." Alex doubtfully grunted acceptance of the idea.

He had been invited, on local Home Shopping Network television the next day to talk about Soft Tough. The conversation he had with his wife was fresh on his mind and the fear of going into the red was giving him the chills. The lights went on, the cameras rolled into position, and the director called for action. The host asked Alex about Soft Tough and he began to talk about Soft Tough's efficacy, the molecular structure, the biodegradable nature, the FDA approvals etc. Then, he realized that the eyes of his host and crew began to glaze over and the director began to yawn. For a moment Alex's mind went blank. Then the host addressed him with concern, "Mr. Reyes, is everything alright?" and he had a big reawakening. "Oh, yeah, I am sorry. Say, instead of talking about the efficacy, the molecular structure, the biodegradable nature, the FDA approvals, etc., for Soft Tough why don't I show you how it works?" "Sure!" responded the host.

Alex quickly unscrewed the bottle of Soft Tough in front of him and took a few large gulps. The host, the camera crew, and the director almost jumped off their seats in shock. Alex smiled and said, "Even though Soft Tough is the toughest and meanest cleaner of engines and machinery, it is as soft as a baby's touch to humans because it is made of all natural materials and is totally harmless. I dare anyone watching out there to prove me wrong."

He closed the TV interview smiling cheek to cheek but with a queasy feeling in his stomach. The following day, he did feel a bit sick but his office phones would not stop ringing. Within weeks the inventory in his warehouse was emptied out and Detox's Soft Tough was on the roll as a brand and a viable product.

In the ensuing months Alex Reyes learned and mastered the art of engagement through the use of metaphors and realized the power of storytelling in pitching products and services. You are probably thinking, "*But I don't make industrial cleaning products that are potable.* In that case, show examples of how good your nuts and bolts are or tell stories about how your nuts and bolts hold together the biggest bridges and skyscrapers in the markets you serve.

Note: This is a fictionalized story that has Truth at its core—the truth that stories sell better than overloaded, left-brain data.

Here is another true example of storytelling, online and on social media, which generated awareness, built large groups of followers, and acquired thousands of loyal customers.

A Story::: Bugsay White Water Rafting

A few years ago, the Department of Tourism and Foreign Affairs of the Philippines, launched a promotional campaign called, *It's More Fun in the Philippines*, which created a lot of visual stories and videos of how much fun it was to travel in the Philippines. The campaign picked up a lot of praise and traction from the press and public alike because of its simplicity and open-endedness. People from all walks of life began to log on, look up, 'Like', and share their own pictures, videos, and stories of having fun in the Philippines. It was a great model for digital storytelling and story-sharing through social media and other platforms.

At about that same time a group of young Filipino businessmen and friends went on a holiday to Cagayan de Oro, in the southern part of the Philippines, where white water rafting was the thing to do. Upon getting to Cagayan de Oro they noticed that the sport wasn't getting much attention from visiting foreigners and Filipinos alike. Because of their love for the sport and for their country, they decided to invest in white water rafting. Soon, they pooled together some funds and bought the handful of white water rafting service providers in Cagayan de Oro and turned them into one business, which they decided to manage themselves. The little outfit came with a few boats, a handful of experienced raftering guides, and the license to operate such a business in the Philippines.

Within months of buying into that outfit they began to build their fun little business into a brand and gave it some system and structure. They made new signs and several banners and billboards. They painted their venues, their boats, oars, safety jackets, and hats. Their brand's theme color of blue took form on all of these and on their logo that was made visible on many websites and everywhere else they could possibly display it.

They dressed up their staff and their rafting guides in their trademark blue. They put up their website, created short and exciting videos, wrote multiple blogs, invited friends and family, and formed their own fan pages on strategically chosen social sites. They began the gradual, steady process of carefully and deliberately promoting their love for the sport through their business which they called Bugsay White Water Rafting.

Direct invitations were sent and free rides and lessons were given to select guests and high-network individuals. Their ethical intentions and sincere efforts began to snowball and gather momentum. Soon the crowds began to fly in, local celebrities dropped by, and bloggers popped up. They all began to create a huge buzz - for free - about the fun they were having in the Philippines with the Bugsay White Water Rafting group from the city of Cagayan de Oro.

The whole country began gushing about white water rafting as if it were a new sport just discovered after Bugsay brought it into the limelight. All other white water rafting services in Cagayan de Oro followed Bugsay's strategy but they were way behind and could not catch up. Bugsay White Water rafting company had firmly emblazoned their story on the skies of Cagayan de Oro and the sport of white-water rafting.

Part owner, Professor Jay Bernardo, of the Asian Institute of Management in the Philippines, knew the power behind storytelling, and he knew how to connect, engage and influence a large mass of people through social media. He did not have to start with,

"Once upon a time..." They just described and shared the truth and created images that allowed their audience to connect the dots and fill in the empty spaces in the conversation. Building a story turned into a mammoth marketing-and-selling tool for white-water rafting in the Philippines.

Today, Bugsay still surfs and rules the waters of Cagayan de Oro and continues to make the Philippines a more fun place to visit.

3 Sourcing stuff for stories

The million dollar question is how? How do we make up stories? How do we create stories? Where in the name of Dickens do we fill in our own great expectations for telling stories and changing the world?

Every language has its own romance and its own idiosyncrasies, and the cultures behind our languages carry some very interesting idioms and sayings. An old Indian saying goes thus, "*Ghaas ke andhe ko har jagah hariyali hi dikhai deti hai.*" A literal translation of that is, "One who is blinded with the love for grass, sees green everywhere."

If you are blinded by the love of stories, then they are everywhere. There are stories in the way a child chuckles at the sight of you. Stories can be found while swinging by the drive-through window of McDonalds. There are millions of stories in how children play, how people work, and how bridges and buildings are built by individuals with great vision. All this is possible because there is truth and life to be found in all these little interactions. Our eyes just need to get attuned to noticing these daily wonders and our minds will step up and repaint the pictures with roses, rainbows and rhythm.

Long ago, someone somewhere set out to change the world. He said the answer to a better world was in changing oneself from the inside. He was an insightful storyteller, this gentleman, and he was lovingly called the "Mahatma." So, before we get on the bus to shop for stories in the marketplace, we have to first rummage through the ruins, pathways, and revelations of our own lives. We have to first, look within in order to come up with juicy, relevant material to write stories with.

On an individual level, nothing works better than looking at our own experiences for creating stories. When we pick up some meat and some vegetables from the marketplace of our mind, we are then totally familiar with the story's setting. We are also totally conversant with the context and "*mais oÙi!*" We recognize the characters well. Stories and examples from our own lives are way more convincing than stories and examples from other people's lives. Whenever leaders indulge in inspiring others, they usually tell a story from their lives and personal experiences—and tell it humbly. Our stories identify, define, and distinguish us and they leave an unforgettable impression on others.

At the organizational level, examples of past successes, best practices, and stories that have given birth to the business work very well. In the US, stories of corporations like General Electric, Ford Motor Company, Disney, Wal-Mart, and Apple have had an impact on businesses, globally. In Asia, companies like Maybank from Malaysia, Infosys from India, and the Ayala Group of Companies from the Philippines have become folklore and legends of their own. Those who work and are involved with such companies know—at an intuitive and subjective level—exactly who they are, what their guiding values are, and which direction to navigate the ships of their organizations daily. Such harmony of thought (read synchronicity) does not come about from studying company financial reports or reading their policy manuals. It comes together because of tradition, culture, and a strong bond at the visceral level.

Searching for Story Materials

Your ways of finding stuff for stories are:

1. **Recall real life personal experiences and critical incidents.**

Take a drive down memory lane and remember incidents that were pleasing to you, sounds that rang through your heart. Recall moments of tenderness and excitement in your life. Look at old pictures, scrapbooks, even yearbooks. Light conversations about those pictures and those sounds with family and friends will help you recall the stories related to them. Perhaps if they are still around, the people in those pictures can help you recapture and recreate those moments in story form.

2. **Talk about organizational successes and best practices.**

Organizations are very similar to individuals. When delving into the past and into your organization's performance, list down your business successes. Then, do another list, this time, of reasons for those successes. What was the environment like, what was the economy like, and what was the socio political atmosphere at that time? What were you doing right? Who were your leaders? How did you feel about your teams and co-workers? Give all these details a shake-up and bring them to life. Compare them to what is happening today and you will have hit pay-dirt when it comes to collecting stuff for stories.

3. Draw from books or history or the news.

When using ideas which are not from your own lives to create stories, effort is needed to create relevance. Make sure that the stories do not offend any caste, color or creed. Make sure that when you convert these ideas to recreate and retell stories, you verify and attribute the source and you clarify the usage and copyright.

It is very important to do a lot of parallel and relevant research for all the ideas and ingredients you acquire for creating and retelling stories. Why? If the authenticity of the data and the simple truth that you are putting across through those stories is challenged, you can then substantiate the message and stand behind your authority.

When using material from external sources, make an effort to remember details. Don't simply display them. Stories are not sharp-edged and geometric but if a part is totally missing and there are no cues for the audience to imagine and recreate it, then your stories, however true, will not hold water. Your delivery will lack the intensity and the engagement that storytelling brings. Remember the essentials by heart. A story sinks into mere linear data when the storyteller has to add, "Let me get back to you on that detail. I am not too sure about it." In storytelling being unsure about certain details just doesn't cut it.

A story needs to become a living, breathing, and fiercely malleable thing inside your mind. That is how you can share and narrate with gusto, with magic, and with impact that blows your audience away. Here's a little story that I have loved and shared for many a decade. It still stirs up warm memories of my youth and the gentle lessons that I learned in those days.

A Story: Sir Fresh Air

It is also said that the meek shall inherit the earth. By meek they don't mean small and scared but someone who is kind, forgiving and most of all, humble. I respect this value and one incident in my life has made it a permanent part of my life.

It was 1969 and I was in my shorts. Yes please, you may take a moment to visualize me in my shorts. Spider legs!

I used to study in a Zoroastrian school, in India, called the Sardar Dastur Hoshang Boy's High School. In those days, hardly twenty years after the British rule, it still carried the Khaki culture. Kids wore Khaki uniforms and several teachers would dress in starched suits with safari-type, hard hats to go with it. The school campus was the size of ten football fields and had wooden buildings like military barracks. In summer the winds blew strong and dusty while in winter the skies were misty till noon.

Several teachers were of the Zoroastrian faith, some were Hindus, and only one of them was a Christian. Mr.

Arputharaj was stout, dark-skinned with Dravidian features. He used to pat his curly, black hair down with pomade and his most outstanding feature was a smile that could be seen a mile away. He taught us Science, English, and Mathematics. He was kind, funny, and always forgiving. And because of his nature, he was always at the receiving end of jokes and pranks.

Being a Christian teacher who taught Science, he'd often be seen marching the corridors of the school with the Bible, Darwin's "The Origin of Species," a blackboard eraser, and a box of chalks by his side. The moment he'd enter a class, he'd demand the windows be thrown open to let in fresh air. He used to pronounce fresh air with flair...fresh aaiyr! And, because of this the boys nicknamed him "Sir, Fresh Aiyr!"

One summer day, Sir, Fresh Air, walked into class sans his brilliant smile but with a look that was distant and pensive. With the eraser, he wiped the big blackboard clean once, twice and until it was black, shiny. With his chalk, he then placed a dot, plumb in the center of the blackboard. Slowly, he turned to the class and stated that we'd be studying Astronomy today and eased himself silently in a chair and stared straight ahead, still pensive and distant.

The boys went wild. "What's that, Sir?", "Is that Astronomy, Sir?", "Is that fresh air, Sir?" He did not react nor respond. The boys continued heckling but he stayed silent and distant. The boys didn't know how to carry on. You cannot continue teasing a person who does not respond. The room turned silent and the silence grew such that a pin, if dropped, would be heard miles away.

Outside the windows of our classroom, hot dust from the playground swirled around, the wind rustled hoarsely among the trees. Sounds of boys talking and shouting in other classrooms seeped into our air through the thick brick walls of buildings built during the British Raj in India. Wooden doors and windows banged away mercilessly in the wind but nothing dared shatter the silence that engulfed our little class, held in a trance by Sir Arputharaj.

After what seemed like a millennium, Sir Fresh Air stood up and began to speak.

"Imagine!" he said.

"Imagine that the blackboard and all the space beyond is the universe. Recognize that the universe has thousands of galaxies and that little dot in the centre is the galaxy that we live in, our Milky Way."

"Imagine," he continued "that within that dot, which is our galaxy, lays our Solar System and within that Solar System is our Sun, the Planets with their moons and our Earth. Within our planet Earth is our country, our hometown and this school room with all of us inside it." "All of that," he went on "is within the dot and more. Yet, we live a life that is filled with pride, distrust and hate."

With a long sigh and still pensive, Sir Fresh Air, slowly sat down. The silence in the room took over again. Outside, the wind still howled and the dust still blew. The boys in the class didn't know what struck them. A while ago they were top of the heap and now they felt puny and negligible in their own minds. With a stroke of his chalk, the Bible-toting, stout, funny brown man with a dazzling smile shattered our egocentric worlds and left us with a lesson in humility that would last us a lifetime.

Yes, it is a true story and it never fails to help me get a right perspective on things and the Truth in the Story is a permanent part of my life.

Storytelling Genres, Five

After you begin to trust the dream-creating and dream-achieving power of stories and storytelling and become addicted to looking out for sources in putting together and telling stories, you will also realize that each one of us homes in towards a certain style of storytelling, a certain genre. This is based on our personal character and styles

The world of literature offers many forms and ways of putting across a message using various genres. For our purpose of creating and driving organizational change today, this book, the HeART of STORY, looks at a few genres of storytelling.

1. Stories that Inspire

We can do all we might on the outside to change people and change the world we live in, but we know change can only be initiated from the inside. Mahatma Gandhi was right when he said, "Be the change that you want to bring about." As leaders and storytellers, we need to make all efforts to light that fire within others to help them change and to help them change the world they live in. This is inspiration.

In stories that inspire, the storyteller need not preach, need not teach, and need not paint himself the hero or the role model for others to emulate and be inspired by. In stories that inspire, one needs to be highly sensitive and knowledgeable about the human psyche and what drives and empowers it. The storyteller needs be extremely creative in weaving together a tale that rubs together the two twigs of example and emotion to create a spark and bring forth bright flames of action and achievement.

2. Stories that Educate

Educational stories may be about the "why" of things. To differentiate them from inspirational and thought-provoking stories that talk about deeper reasons and values, they need to be a bit more about the "how" of things where people can pick up cues and examples of how things are done–how they are executed, analyzed, understood, and evaluated for improving knowledge and skills.

Enlightened teachers know and often use the power of stories when creating examples and case studies of work and business practices in order to untangle the thinking process and improve performance and productivity. The essence of all storytelling is narration and engagement, but stories that educate focus a lot more on knowledge development.

3. Stories of Adventure and Courage

The movie world is filled with tons of this kind of story-telling. This is the ultimate story of an ordinary character faced with extraordinary circumstances. It talks about how she breaks all bonds, rises from the shackles, vanquishes her foes, and cuts through all obstacles between her and the achievement of her dreams—the freedom of her spirit and emotions.

In this genre, it is important that the context and setting are described vividly and the characters are swashbuckling-ly dynamic, unique, and full of fun. When you create and share this story, throwing in a horse, a hat, and an extremely ugly-mean villain will add a sprinkle of sugar and spice that is needed for such story-telling.

4. Stories of Emotions and Drama

Stories of drama also flourish in the movies. This genre's stories usually put across a message about how to deal with people and how to build and sustain healthy relationships. Personal stories of emotional turmoil that spring forth during corporate team building and bonding events help resolve issues and remove barricades to organizational growth.

The characterizations in this genre need not be excessively dramatic or unique. This works best with characters from the workplace, from family, or the average person on the street. What is important here are the details of dialogue, the play on emotions, and the sensitivity of scripts used for re-enacting scenarios.

The CBS series, *Undercover Boss*, is a great example of this kind of storytelling. Have a look:

http://www.cbs.com/shows/undercover_boss/

5. Stories of Humor and Happiness

For the purpose of inspiring, educating, and driving change all stories must—traditionally and technically—have humor and happiness intertwined into the plot and into its opening and ending. Otherwise, these stories will be unable to deflect the left brain's resistance to new information and will fail to inspire.

One quick, easy, and very powerful tip for using humor is to make yourself, your team, and your side, look and play the buffoon and the victim in the story. Then narrate the story from a third person perspective and say it as if you were talking about your own silliness behind your own back.

One word of caution: refrain from making light of someone's beliefs or race. That is not at all funny. It is insulting and humiliating. My previous book, The HeART of Humor, tools you up with seven wordplay techniques on how to improve your humor and thus, your happiness quotient.

4

STRUCTURING STORIES

This book would be doing a disservice if it claimed that there is one specific way to structure a story. There are no structures, but there are infinite ways to structure storytelling. Every approach to telling a story can be innovated. Since there are no rules that have been laid down for measuring the success of our attempts at innovating stories, then let us assume there are also no rules for measuring our failures in that arena. Once you get the hang of connecting with your audience, holding them in a trance, and changing their minds, then you can juggle the storytelling methods and structures any which way you want.

The story of Red Riding Hood can be retold from the wolf's perspective making him the hero and the protagonist. It can be retold from the lumberjack's perspective making him the hero. It can simply open up with, "What big teeth you have, Grandmother!" and tell the whole story as a flashback. It can finally open up with the little girl, her grandmother and the lumberjack walking away with hats made of wolf skin. And, if the genre of this little story was not a fairy tale with a happy ending, we could let the wolf walk away with a well-filled stomach. Growl, growl!

The point is the structure of a story should never be created in a linear way. Describing any story as structured just does not cut it. A story can be interesting, exciting, funny, happy, scary, mind-blowing, out-of-this-world, romantic, tragic…anything except nicely and properly structured. A nicely-and-properly-structured story would be a mathematical equation, not a story. How a story is fluffed together is like how you would hold together mist, clouds, a shoal of fishes, or cotton candy. Like cotton candy with its lightness, sweetness, color, and lack of form, a story can be bitten into from any angle or direction. It can be plucked into from any end and nibbled away until you pop the last delicious bite into your mouth, and then declare it, "The End."

Open Space Technology Approach

In the world of organizational development, leaders need to continuously figure out what they are doing right, where future opportunities lie, how people can stay engaged and happy, and how to assess the changes of a constantly evolving world, so that the organization can move forward confidently, peacefully, and holistically. To help leaders figure out answers to such questions, organizational developmental consultants apply a method of facilitation known as the *Open Space Technology*. OST, as it is referred to, was created nearly 30 years ago by a gentleman named Harrison Owen. The essence of OST is it strives to de-structure learning and dialogue. It allows conversations to flow, to grow organically with barely a push or a shove towards a cognitive end. When people from the media and advertising industries hold conferences, they call this similar approach the "Unconference."

Very briefly, here are the guidelines for this approach called *Unconference*, which actually is *Open Space Technology*.

- Whoever comes is the right "people."
- Whenever it starts is the right time.
- Wherever it happens is the right place.
- Whatever happens is the only thing that could have.
- When it's over, it's over.
- Follow the *Law of Two Feet.*

  If at any time during our time together you find yourself in any situation where you are neither

> learning nor contributing, use your two feet, go someplace else. The *Law of Two Feet*, essentially, says: "Don't waste time!" "Keep on moving!" "Keep on adding!"

How this approach relates to storytelling is…

- The story can be told and retold from any character's perspective. It is still a story but it might turn into a different story with a different message.
  You can start a story from any stage in the story and wind and rewind it from there. Your audience will piece the puzzle together and enjoy the complexity and challenge of doing so. The scenario and the setting stay flexible. A story can always be told using a different setting.
- When the story ends, that can be the end or the start of a fresh, new story. Classic story-writers refer to it as letting the story trail off at a beautiful turn and letting the audience's imagination go on wondering.

You have watched movies where you had to figure out whether the hero lived or died. It works! Nicely too! Many Zen stories are like that. They shoot you up into the air and let you float away to wherever you wish.

- Finally, the *Law of Two Feet* translates into keeping your story moving on into the next frame, into the next scene. If we drone on in our storytelling or story-writing then our audience will surely and

> quickly die upon our disappointingly boring shoulders.

Thus to summarize "Structuring," this book will NOT offer you a framework that looks like a line, a square, or an upside down triangle. Instead, it will flex your mind, warm your heart, and stretch your wrist such that you learn to doodle. Doodle so well, in fact, that every squiggle looks like a work of art which gets your message across to the audience who then add their own special meaning to your masterpieces.

Seven Essentials of an Uunstructured Story

Here are the essentials to fluffing together or "doodling" a story into a work of art. When you get a handle on this, you may then take away any of these essentials or add a few of your own. The purpose behind your efforts is to engage, entertain, and hopefully, to educate the world.

1. Choose a Core Truth.

Choose a simple, core truth that you want to put across through story. This truth is also referred to as the theme of the story in literature studies. Examples of simple truth:

> Money can't buy you love.
> Where there's a will, there's a way.
> Actions speak louder than words.

Your story must have a point. One point! When your story has two points then it could imply that you are telling two stories in one. This point that you are making through storytelling must be something you think is important and needs to be brought up between you and your audience.

A long meaningful conversation or a large *Unconference* can have a lot of messages. Most messages can be eventually wrapped together in one direction and integrated in one story. It is important for a story to have one core truth—a core message and a point. It is also important that we veer away from expounding upon clichés and euphemisms.

Trust the Truth, personally.

Like and trust this truth yourself and keep it specific and succinct. Any kind of effort at influencing someone or a group of people is a pitch. It is an effort to sell an idea, a proposal, or a new way of thinking. Now the other truth about life is that you just cannot sell something that you have not genuinely bought into, yourself. Think about it! If you make a big effort to convince someone to use a product that YOU do not trust, would they buy it? No way! No way, Jose! That's because if you don't like it, don't trust it, or are not sure it works, your efforts to push-sell it will not be authentic. It then becomes a lie; not the truth. Remember, stories are truths wrapped in roses, rainbows and rhythm.

When you sell or propose an idea and you don't buy into it, yourself, it creates what is known in the field of Neuro

Linguistic Programming as "incongruence." In incongruence there is a hard battle between our internal thoughts and our external expressions and behavior. People sense it, see it in our nervousness, and hear it in the brittleness of our voices. At a kinesthetic-feeling level it fills them with doubt and suspicion. The worst thing is that we, ourselves,

see it, hear it, and feel it in our sweating palms and parching throats. Lies just do not work.

Tell the truth and keep the truth focused in one direction. Don't be wishy-washy about it. When you keep your eyes, your heart, and your mind locked in one direction towards one goal and one truth, then all the verbal arrows and the non-verbal arrows of your expression will flawlessly and fruitfully hit that singular bulls-eye.

This Truth, depending on the context and the recipients of the story, may or may not be made explicit. Think through and consider the alignment and relevance of the story you choose, with this simple, core Truth. Write it down to let it crystallize in your mind. You will then enjoy wrapping it in roses, rainbows, and rhythm.

Hearing a great story narrated by a master raconteur is as trance-inducing as watching a master juggler throw up a ball, a bottle, and a knife at the same time and then keep them afloat in the air, like magic! The audience really has no idea which one went up first and which one will be coming down last. Listening to a master raconteur tell a great story is as trance-inducing as watching a pizza maker throw up a lump of flour, then roll it, flip it, and swing it around until it lands on the table flattened and ready to walk itself into the oven with cheese and tomatoes trailing right behind it.

The point is the master juggler and the pizza chef both know exactly what they are doing. They know that we the audience will be mesmerized and stay entranced through the process. They know that at the end of their show they will have entertained us and will have turned out a mouth-watering, steaming hot pizza. They do not need to tell us what they are doing or what they will create. We know. We see. We feel. We sense. And we walk away enlightened and gastronomically fulfilled.

Spelling out the message in a story is like explaining the punch line of a good joke. There is no fun in that. It is not participative or inclusive and it is never empowering. In fact, there is a good chance that at the end of it, your audience will respond with, "Duh!"

Work at your story and storytelling such that the message silently evolves, gradually rises, and powerfully lights up the skies in the minds of your audience. Work at it so it fills and fattens their hearts.

2. Cover the Context, Briskly.

Context to a story is what canvass is to a painting. It gives the groundwork and the space upon which the images and the story can be painted. The type of impact a story creates is crucially dependent on the kind of canvass upon which the pictures are painted. Just as we must know what kind of truth we are putting across with the story, we must also know on which kind of canvass that story can be created. The size, the shape, the color, the tilt, and the texture of the canvass are of high importance.

Use a very small canvass and your story will fall through. Labor though a very large canvass and your story could become weak and leave your audiences dissatisfied.

In building context, we must clearly and succinctly fulfill the answers to questions such as:

Where and when did this happen?

What was the landscape and terrain like where the story occurred?

What was life like during the time of the story?

What were the people like and what were their moods and relationships towards each other?

Which background and beliefs influenced their attitude and behavior?

Be cautious with spending too much time and over-indulging yourself when creating the canvass. It is important and has to be deftly handled, but you have to get on with your stories and hit the ground running. People are more interested in appreciating paintings and in how the paintings

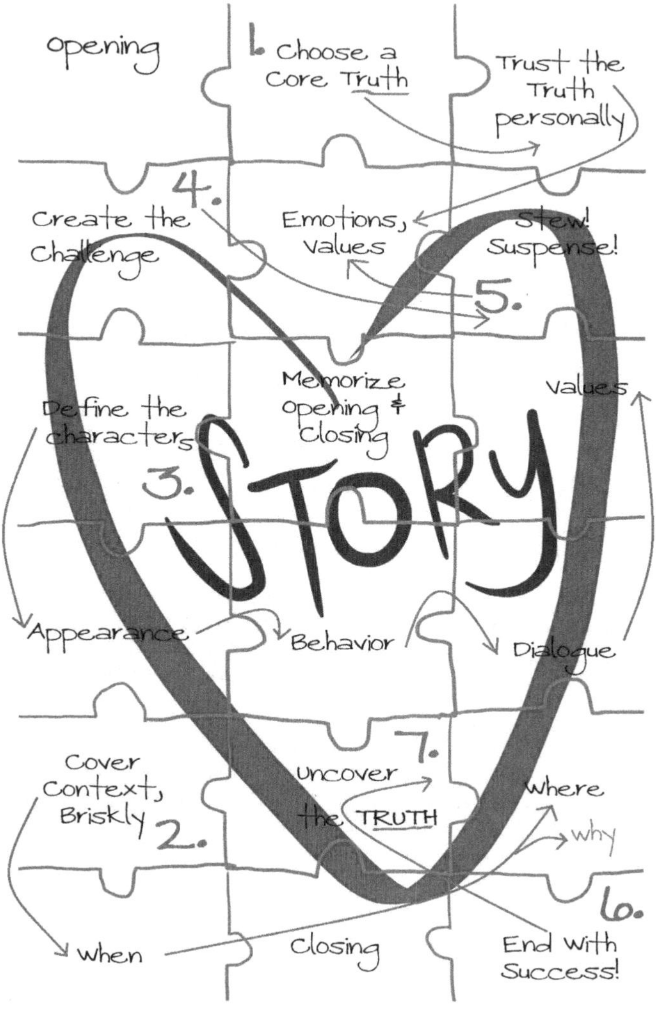

storytelling the order of the context, the character, and the challenge can be played with as long as the storyteller ties all between his opening and closing.

speak to them directly. It is rare for an audience to be taken in and inspired by the canvass alone.

Refrain from overdoing the context-building but be cautious too of leaving out essential details. In either case, your audience may miss out making the connections and your masterpiece, your story may not have effect you intended it to have. Do also make sure to quickly compare and contrast the context of the story with the everyday realities of your audience.

Now here's the deal. It is strongly discouraged that you be totally blunt about your message, like blurting it out loud, *"What I am trying to say here in this story is that money can't buy love!"* The whole process of storytelling becomes highly creative and exciting when we drop gentle cues and hints as to where we are going with the story and how it relates to the realities of life.

Just like in a good Alfred Hitchcock mystery, the audience participates and hangs onto every detail because the picture is slowly, subtly, and slyly being unraveled to them. The audience leans and wants to jump ahead and "get it," or "catch the culprit." It is an edge-of-the-seat kind of participation because both the storyteller and the audience are connecting known and unknown dots together.

When telling the story, relate it to current realities. Describe the hero and compare her to someone the audience knows. Detail the challenge in the story and briskly drop a few words about critical incidents similar to work-life situations.

Pop in and out of these descriptions like you are making masterful strokes with a paint brush. Keep your audience moving, thinking, and feeling with you and with the characters in the story. Remember the *Law of Two Feet* as mentioned earlier and focus on not wasting precious time. Keep on adding and keep the story moving along; otherwise, your audience will walk away from you.

Apply this approach of quickly comparing and contrasting. Your audience will then do the integrating, patching up, linking, and will eventually put together the message themselves. Let them have the pleasure of "getting it" and "catching the culprit" and going "Aha!" when they figure out the simple, core Truth in your story.

Memorize the Opening and the Closing.

Plan ahead and memorize the opening and the closing of your story. Memorizing an interesting beginning is like saying "Open Sesame!" to the minds our listeners. It is the nature of the human mind to open up and to be highly attentive to novel things and fresh ideas. Every time it gets a sniff of a new idea, a new concept, or a new beginning its antennae of curiosity goes up. Its senses and attentiveness perks up. To make the most of this nature of the human mind, good storytellers know they must create an interesting, intriguing opening. The more intriguing and dramatic the opening is, the more widely receptive the human mind is. In some schools of thought, this is known as the Law of Primacy. And once the human mind opens up, it is like a parachute that is difficult to close.

The mind is high on curiosity, keen on expectations and thus, also quick on rejection. Take for example this opening, "It is not power that corrupts, but fear. Fear of losing power corrupts those who wield it and fear of the scourge of power corrupts those who are subject to it..." These words were spoken by Aung San Suu Kyi, Noble Peace Prize winner and opposition leader of Myanmar, in her famous *Freedom from Fear* speech in 1990. It is an opening that clamps on the minds of the listeners and keeps them open and wanting more.

Here are some suggestions for Opening stories and Closing stories:

- Get creative with the opening for your stories. Start with a dialogue, an action sequence, or a colorful setting. Describe the angst and the mindset of a character and then start weaving your theme around that opening. Make sure to be clear and quick. Learn it by memory. Memorizing it will allow you to use your tonality and body language to add more impact.

- Decide on a theme and choose an obvious or subtle hook. A theme is the subject matter in the story or its color and environment. A hook is repetition around the theme. It may be a bunch of words, a gesture, or a habit. Every word, every picture, every incident, and dialogue of your story needs to weave in and out this theme. All of them, put together, will crescendo into an exciting and dynamic ending.

- The ending must easily put across the simple Truth; preferably, also implicitly. As you start working your way towards the ending, make sure it is dynamic. Exert the effort to clearly visualize and memorize it. If you have planned the ending well and you have a crystal clear picture of it in your mind, all your other endeavors in the storytelling process will be like rungs to a ladder—a ladder that will lead to a dynamic end with a simple, implicit truth.

3. Define your Characters.

Describe, define and differentiate the characters in the story. Preferably have one hero. Describe her appearance, behavior, and attitude.

"She was strong-boned, grey-haired and had 'I love my son' written all over her."

"She moved around her kitchen with purpose and determination."

"She was whistling as she worked because her son was coming home soon."

Notice that while building characters for your story, you do not just tell; you creatively describe the character. Instead of just "saying" that she was an old woman, you "show" her by painting a word picture. "Her craggy face and greying eyes lit up like a chandelier whenever she thought of her son."

A person's appearance, posture, gait, habits, and the way she thinks and talks are the sketch-lines that display and define the characters we create.

For example:

Dialogue:

"It is not about how hard you hit. It is about how hard you get hit and then get up and go for it again."

Action:

"He slowly placed his thumb and forefinger on his pointed, unshaven chin and began to think."

Reactions

"She blushed at his compliments and gently lowered her eyes."

Relationships:

"The way he stood around his mother expressed a protective and caring nature."

Situations:

"Every time her son fell and wounded himself, she'd get dizzy, feel faint and gasp for air rather than reach out to the child and attend to his wounds."

4. CREATE THE CHALLENGE

Create the challenge and complexity around the life of the main character. This is also known as the plot of the story. It is an answer to, "What happens or what happened?"

"Wait; there was no cake-flour at home!"

"The son she loved would be home in an hour. She'd promised to be ready with the cake when he got home."

"She had no money and her nearest neighbor was miles away. She felt trapped and helpless."

An interesting and intriguing plot will keep your audiences engaged and hungry for more at every step of the story. Struggles on the surface can be built around physical, financial, relational, and other challenges. In essence, they are emotions and are usually about:

Values: What is right?

Purpose: What am I doing?

Identity: Who am I?

Although on the surface, the hero of your story is battling with physical, financial, and social challenges, she is usually fighting bigger internal demons. Take any of the massively successful animated moves like *Beauty and the Beast, the Lion King, Kung fu Panda, Brave, and Frozen.* The heroes and characters are all fighting physical and societal battles but deep inside they are involved in bigger quests such as:

Who am I?

Why am I the way I am?

Why can't I let go?

Make sure your stories also put across such unspoken challenges of your characters and thus, of your audience. Stew the struggle and steam the characters

"She dug through the pantry and found flour for the bread."

"Then she noticed there was no wood in the oven or at home. Outside, it had begun to rain."

"I love my son,' she said, desperate and driven, as she began to chop down the wooden chairs in her home."

Whatever external and internal battles your heroes might be facing, make sure to expound upon them. Make certain that they stew in the struggle and sink in the quagmire of fear, anxiety, and guilt for a while. As your characters go through this process in your story, your audience will identify with them and resonate with your characters' feelings. They will work on the challenges in their own lives and will find hope and strength to resolve them while participating in your creations.

5. Elevate the Suspense

"Time was running out. She chopped up the chairs for firewood, faster and harder."

At this stage the audience is highly engaged and mentally rummaging through similar experiences of their own. In their minds, they might be going, *What in heaven's name is she doing?* Exaggerate certain parts while underplaying others. This is where your audience's imagination gets stretched and strained.

No matter how often and how many times people hear and read stories where the hero wins, they just cannot help but get anxious over the fate of the characters they identify with in the story. The fun and the engagement lie in stretching these feelings a bit more and in not coming up with solutions right away. Working up the challenges, staying engrossed, and vicariously living the fears and feelings of the characters helps the audience work through and soothe their own troubles. This is the beauty of participating in a story.

6. End, always with Success!

Traditionally, the hero always overcomes the challenges and succeeds in her journeys. The simple, core truth, "Where there's a will there's a way" is transferred.

The story might be of a mother baking a cake, but it intrinsically also answers-

Values: What is right?

Purpose: What am I doing?

Identity: Who am I?

7. Uncover the Core Truth in Story

Perhaps in the end, the hero does not come out victorious. Maybe he dies. Maybe the villain gets the girl and the gold. Whichever way the story ends, the message your story is putting across must get through.

The message is usually a truth, a virtue, or a strength; therefore, whoever wins must in some way be good and virtuous and thus, become the hero.

Your job as an effective storyteller is let this truth be understood, hopefully accepted and then lived out in the real lives of your audience.

5

Serving the Stories with a Sizzle

For the same reasons behind the recommendation of using your own examples, experiences and anecdotes in story creation, we must refrain from telling and selling stories when they have not yet come together. We should not serve a story before it has become rich, thick and creamy within our own minds.

A Story: A Hole-In-One

When an incident occurs—say you hit a hole-in-one while you are out alone on the golf course— you call up your brother in Kalamazoo and excitedly tell him the facts. He responds with a "Harrumph, blah, baloney!" That makes you a little disconcerted. You wonder what it is that you did wrong. Why doesn't your very own brother believe you?

A week later you call up your younger sister and chat with her. This time, you start slowly. You begin by getting over the courtesies and by clearing away the desktop of her constantly active mind. You then start with, "Hey Sis, you won't believe what happened to me here in Jakarta a week ago!" She responds with, "Of course I'll believe you Bro, you never lie. What happened?" This time you make some headway with your story of a hole-in-one and your audience, your sweet little sister, now responds with, "That's wonderful Bro! You are amazing. Bye now!" Armed with this little success plus the memory and the excitement of making a hole-in-one, you are now privy to some very powerful secrets about storytelling.

A month later, at an evening of cocktails and networking with business buddies, you start with, "You have absolutely no idea, and you just can't imagine what happened to me last April!" All your friends lean in and peer down your face and you begin, "It was one of those pink-blue mornings on the Rivera and I was alone, alone as Adam must have been before Eve." Slowly and surely you are raisin their curiosity, raising expectations and briskly building context. Then you go ahead and tell them the story. That evening you become the toast of the town. You walk out of the business meeting—a legend in your own mind and a legend on Main Street. You wrapped your Truth in Story and you became awesome in the eyes of your friends!

There! You have it! That is how to tell stories that sizzle.

The Five Steps to a Sizzle

So, way before truth turns into a story and then hopefully into a legend, it has to steam in your mind and stew in your active thoughts. It has to first simmer in your thoughts and then again in action during conversations.

It is the same with social and organizational stories that have built the culture to drive constructive change and to bring about real and lasting transformations. Within organizations, the stories steam and simmer in individual minds, but they also simmer in the corridors, at the water cooler, and in board rooms. Finally they consolidate, integrate, and resonate for a long time, bringing extended periods of growth and prosperity for the company.

When telling stories in any format or media, and especially in the spoken word, practice the following habits:

1. **CHURN IT AROUND IN YOUR HEAD FIRST.**

    - Again, knead and push the story around in your head as many times as you can.
    - Review it so many times that you can see, hear, and feel it from many perspectives.
    - Visualize it from the storyteller's perspective.
    - Feel and enact it from one of the character's point of view.
    - Make an effort to feel it mentally as your audience might.

2. **EMOTE THE DRAMA THROUGH EXPRESSIONS.**

- Make sure the joy and sorrow of the characters surface on your face.
- Let your eyes acknowledge and analyze the emotional transfer to the audience.
- When a point is laid across and accepted by the audience, and they begin to think, think and ponder along with them.

3. **EXPRESS THE DYNAMISM THROUGH YOUR BODY**

- In storytelling you know all the fine details but you are not expressing them all in just words. You are telling the essentials, creating images, and delivering the dialogues.
- Your eyes, gestures, and actions also communicate and put across a larger portion of the story.
- Step forward to make a point. Step back to let it sink in. Manage and control the stage as you speak. It is called blocking—moving from one scene to another, from one state of mind to another, from one character to another, and when your point of view has been expressed.

4. **PLAY WITH YOUR VOICE**

- Speak slowly and enunciate well. Speed up only when the scene requires it. Percolate, power up, and project your voice. Like a singer does, pump up air from the depths of the diaphragm, create rhythm, and project by increasing your voice volume by several decibels.

- Change tones and accents if you are speaking the lines of different characters in the story.
- Maintain a warm, friendly, personal voice between you, the storyteller and your audience.

5. Pause often. Pause for effect.

- When you appear to be in deep thought as to the state of mind of the characters, when you reflect upon the message, or as you realize its impact right there in front of the audience, then the audience also feels, reflects, and realizes the impact. A pause is a powerful soundless statement.
- Pause and allow your thinking to be visible to the audience. Pause before you begin the story. Pause after you pitch a line. Pause at commas and pause longer at periods. Slow down and pause at twists and turns in the story. Like Shakespearean actors Al Pacino and Anthony Hopkins, pause with power, pause often and pause in style.

A Story: when in the Philippines...

On that day she was celebrating 30 years of good and happy living in the Philippines. At about 10 am she drove into the central business district of Makati to draw some cash from the automated teller machine at Citibank. Parking was, as usual, hard to find so she put on her emergency blinkers, squeezed in ahead of a large, already parked, white van and ran into the bank's lobby hoping to step out quickly.

A few steps into the large, classy lobby of the bank she sensed it but didn't pay any attention to the fact that there was an eerie silence. There also seemed to be no people around. At the ATM machine she shoved in her card, punched in her numbers, and took the cash that poured out. On her mind was her illegally parked car on the street outside and the thought that it might get hauled away by the police.

As she was about to turn and make a run for the door, from the corner of her eye she saw a woman in red crouched behind the service counter, hiding. The woman with her finger on her lips was whispering something to her in Filipino. "*Weird people*" my friend thought and glanced to her left. This time, she saw two men spread-eagled on the floor of the bank. "*It's getting crazier*!" She thought to herself and moved on.

She was unconscious of it but all this while, the loud speaker in the lobby was announcing something in Filipino.

A chill ran up her spine when she heard her car plate numbers being read and by instinct, she leaped and crouched behind the counter where the lady in red was hiding. Through a choppy, whispered, difficult conversation, the lady in red was able to explain to her that there was a small car with blinking lights blocking a big white get-away van of the guys who were currently robbing the bank. When my friend, who had been living in the Philippines for over 30 years, looked up and around she did realize that there were strange looking men walking around with huge guns in their hands.

That day, the American, non-Filipino-speaking consultant from the Asian Development Bank who up to then had lived a good and happy life in the fun-loving and warm Philippines, lay cold for a long while on the floor of Citibank in Makati.

Until news of the robbery hit town the next day, none of her family and friends believed her story of being an accidental hero during a major bank heist in her host country where she didn't speak the language.

"Open-Story-Close "for Sales

Master salesmen and sales consultants will agree when I say that the traditional sales process, like the wheel, can no longer be re-invented. It can be improved and it can be modified, but it cannot be changed in essence. Individuals and industries break up the sales cycle into a 9-step, a 7-

Sales Process

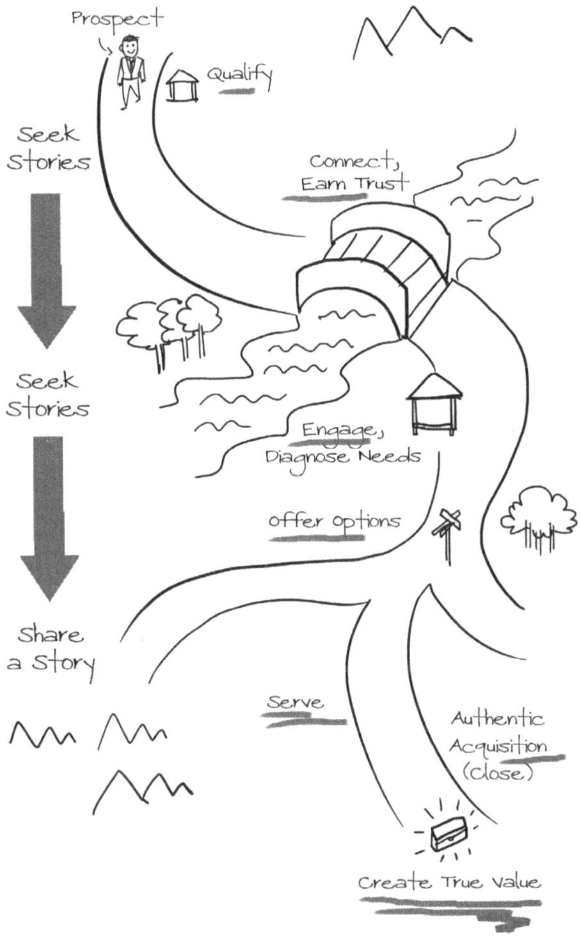

In a sales pitch, stories work like grease does on wheels. And, customer stories give you insights into their real needs.

step, a 5-step, or a 3-step process. Let us say the process, by natural law, consists of prospecting, qualifying, analyzing needs, presenting options, handling objections, adjusting, and then closing a deal. When simplified, it is a matter of connecting and engaging and then, ethically and tenderly influencing your potential customers to buy from you.

It is common knowledge—and research substantiates this—that people have a psychological resistance to being "sold to." But they love the thought of having "bought" something of their own accord, of their own free will from their own informed choice. Why is there such resistance? The underlying neuro-psychological reason is always the same. It is fear— fear of the unknown, fear of the salesperson who is practically a stranger, fear of inexperience (their own and maybe the salesperson's) and fear of losing what they possess, which is usually money.

We know stories and storytelling gives us an unfair advantage of being able to duck and deflect such fear-based resistance.

But no matter how long or short the steps of your sales process might be, after you complete the stages of finding a prospect, establishing his needs, and putting together a valuc-crcating solution, you could still mcct high walls of resistance from prospects whom you are unable to convrt into clients.

That is the time to consider if this selling attitude is purely left brain and logic driven. That is a good time to tell them a story. This does not mean we do not tell stories before or after then. It means we. need to tell a story that pivots their thoughts from ground up.

At the closing stage, slowly and subtly share a story of a similar case or of a parallel scenario where the buyer hesitated and lost an opportunity, where a buyer was reluctant and prices moved up, where a buyer eased back and invested in a wrong location or product. With your story, make the benefits visible, viable, and easily achievable. With your story, build a sense of personal urgency.

By this process, you will create the space for your buyers to make their own decision. You will create the space where they feel safe to think through all the options in a whole-brain manner. In the end, THEY will own the decision and will feel that THEY have made the purchase. In THEIR minds, you played a helpful but minor role.

A word of caution: great stories and greater storytelling may clinch you deals but they do not necessarily win you happy, loyal-for-life customers. Good stories and good storytelling abilities need to be backed by truth, by ethical delivery of service, and by the constant endeavor to innovate and improve in order to consistently impress your customers.

6

Serving Stories with a Sizzle and a Salsa

Although stories and storytelling by itself is a visceral and emotionally participative activity, advanced storytellers can raise the bar on this interaction by employing the following strategies.

Five Steps to Salsa

1. Employ rhetorical questions to build context.

> *Does anyone know the name of the highest peak in the Himalayas?*
>
> *Any idea what language they speak in Brazil?*
>
> *Which month of 1989 did they break down the Berlin wall?*

Regardless of whether you know the answer or not, use questions every now and then. Questions will make your audience sit up. They may offer only quick, one-word answers but they will get on the same page and then become interested in where you, the storyteller, will be taking them.

Be cautious when using very broad and open-ended questions as these could navigate your storytelling ship into unknown territories. You can use open-ended questions if you are building the story in the moment and the audience members are your co-creators of the story. This requires extremely advanced skills in the art and discipline of improvisation such as those employed by stand-up comedians and other spoken-word artists.

These five ideas for serving your stories with a sizzle and salsa that I am sharing with you are inspired by the art and discipline of improvisation. At the end of these five steps, I will share some insights into improvisation but for corporate storytellers like us, it is prudent to use closed questions for improved interaction and engagement. Closed questions will keep your audiences active and allow them to offer one-word or short-sentence responses.

2. **Choose audience members to represent characters in the story.**

So let's say Abe Lincoln was tall and gaunt just like Stewart over here in the front.

Corrie, had you been around in the 19th Century, Florence of Nightingale might have looked, walked, and talked like you.

We might say that Gandhi probably was the size and shape of Ben over in that corner.

This expedites and adds a point of comparison for building characters in the story. This technique also adds light benign humor and increases audience engagement. Every time you mention the character during your storytelling, a live visual pops up in the minds of your audience and creates a sense of reality and fun. A well-prepared, professional storyteller will make it a point of getting permission in advance from the audience member whom he plans to use as an anchor for creating his characters. This is good storytelling etiquette and prevents misunderstandings later.

When you involve them and the listeners, "get in the zone," then the storytelling becomes a dance, a salsa.

A story: 10,000 to 9,000 Things

In 1971 San Franciso, on the corner of 26th and South Van Ness, a handsome cable car gripman on a motorcycle plunges under a laundry truck, breaks his pelvis, and crushes an elbow as spilled gas ignites and chars 65% of his body. After months of healing and recovering from such an incident, former school dropout W. Mitchell moves to another town, earns a Master's Degree, becomes Mayor, turns into an environmentalist, and makes scores of wise investments that earn him millions.

Four years later in Colorado, after having struggled back into complete recovery, the same gentleman's turbocharged Cessna takes a plunge that breaks his back and legs forever. Again, after years of therapy and treatments, W. Mitchell, hops onto a wheelchair and takes to the road telling his story of *It's Not What Happens to You but What you Do About it*, to the world.

In the decades that follow he travels to over 30 countries spreading his message of hope and inspiration. During this period he also gets invited to speak and present at the White House on five different occasions. On one occasion, President Clinton introduces him as the person who could do 10,000 things before his injuries, can now do 9,000 things, and feels good about doing them.

Today, as a powerful and inspiring international speaker, he has acquired a unique style of telling his story. He begins by describing the day in 1971 San Francisco and then turns to a male member in the audience and says, “You, dressed as an Ambulance Driver, lifted me up in your arms and ran me to the hospital. You saved my life.” He then turns to a young female member of the audience and says, “You, Beverly, taught me how to get off the wheelchair and onto the sofa and from the sofa back onto the wheelchair.”

This method and style of storytelling keeps the audience spellbound and awed not just by the images he paints but the fact that he, literally, lifts the soul and the spirit of random members of the audience and makes them play the role in a movie made of words and sounds. I would say the method sizzles and sears the message. If one was once able to do 10,000 things before a serious debilitating accident, then by the power of his will, he can continue dong 9,000 things even after such devastating losses.

3. Hand the hook to the audience.

- Every time the mother does something about the challenges she faces in the story, have the audience answer as to what is ringing true in her heart, “*I love my son, I love my son!*”

- As soon as she pulled the cake out of the oven, the aroma made her think….pause… “*I love my son, I love son!*” offers the whole audience in tandem to the story.

To employ this technique, it is crucial to build an escalating level of engagement with the audience. In addition, the lines you "hand" them to throw into your storytelling must also be funny, must deepen the character in the story, and must have a certain rhythm to them.

4. **Pretend to forget parts or names or locations in the story.**

    - Advanced storytellers sometimes deliberately go, "Now, where was I?" or "What was the name of that forgetful US president during the 80s?"

- This is fun because audiences so want you to succeed and tell a good story that they lean in and make special efforts to fill you in and help you. Remember, storytelling is organic, contagious, and a group effort. It is synergy in action.

This technique is a creative combination of asking questions and handing lines to the audience to share and offer. This makes you the bumbling but interesting storyteller, and that is exactly the strategy and the purpose behind this idea.

Years ago, I heard this story about a door-to-door bible salesman who would knock on the doors of his prospects and then open up his book samples and brochures. He would mumble words when he introduced himself and would not have any sort of pitch or presentation. He would scratch his head, be uneasy, and look doe-eyed sorry and confused in the presence of his potential customer. His unusual behavior would drive the potential customers crazy and they would grab one of the copies of his Bible and yell at him. "You have no idea, how to sell do you son? Let me show you how!" And they would proceed to show him how and in the process, also buy one (or more copies) to prove their point. He would then happily walk away with one more good book sold.

5. **Tell the story from the point of view of one of the characters in the story.**

This is also known as angle perspective. Here is another angle on the story of *The Little Red Riding Hood.*

Once upon a time there was a dear little girl who was loved by everyone who looked at her but most of all by her grandmother, and there was nothing that she would not have given to the child. Once, she gave her a little riding hood of red velvet, which suited her so well that she would never wear anything else; so she was always called 'Little Red Riding Hood.

Change that to:

Of all the people who love me, I think my grandmother loves me the most. There is nothing in the world she wouldn't give me. One day, she gave me this wonderful velvet riding hood and it was bright red in color. I wore it everywhere all the time and people began to call me, 'Little Red Riding Hood.

By handing the job of telling the story to one of the characters from the story, we make the story a little more ex citing and a little more personal. Obviously, working with stories from the world of business and industry will call for extra creativity and focus, but it can be achieved and it can deliver better results. It does become a lot easier with the use of media like audio, video, or interactive software. In the marketing and advertising arena, this form of storytelling takes the shape of testimonies that create more traction in entrenching brand awareness. Many marketing campaigns have created online caricature characters of their target customer and have used them effectively to tell the stories of their brand and organization.

Improvisation, "Yes, And" the Rules

Now, what exactly is the art and science of improvisation? Think of what a band of jazz musicians do. A jazz band has no leaders, no maestro, and no planned set. Any one of the band members can start strumming or humming a note then another picks it up, changes it a bit, or simply adds to it. They don't reject or exclude any note. They just keep on adding, twisting, turning, and, building until it takes form—any form—and then they celebrate the results. They go with what works and worry little about notes that did not go well or did not jive.

Improvisation artists do the same thing with words, sentences, and stories. They keep on adding, building, supporting, giving, and backing up their partners. Anyone! The goal is not to be hard and fast but to be free-flowing and creative. This is rapid-fire creativity in action that is all positive. There are no put downs, no complaints, no fears, no doubts, no negatives. It all ends up being a lot of fun too.

THE RULES

Improvisation is rapid, supportive creativity in action. It appreciates, it acknowledges, and it constructs. "Improv," as it is called, never doubts, never questions, and never condemns any offer of a thought, a word, or a behavior. It is making things out of what is at hand, out of nothing.

The first, most powerful rule is to learn to respond to any offer or suggestion or idea with a "Yes, and" response. What the "yes" does is accept and what the "and" does is add and build, thus, allowing this interactive creation process to grow and develop. Give this concept some thought. Doesn't every business idea need acceptance, appreciation, and support? This is the ultimate talisman of creativity—to be open and accepting, to support and build.

The other rules are:

1. Whenever you add or build upon an idea, always sustain a sense of play. Play is joyfully doing something in the present moment.

2. Learn to live with ambiguity and failure. Be willing to move on into the unknown, the untested, the never before experienced.

3. Listen. Listen with a deep and honest intention to change—to flex and adapt to the needs of the moment, to the needs of the stakeholders.

4. Improv is a game. Storytelling is a game. Business and life is a game. Games have rules; thus, play the game by the stated or unstated rules.

5. Have fun throughout while adding, listening, failing and playing the game. Have fun and relax.

These are the soft, tender, malleable rules of improvisation when creating and constructing in partnership with others. Similarly, storytelling with a sizzle and salsa is allowing your audience to play an active part in the dance. Your job is to lead or to be led. If your audience stumbles, just smile, support, and move on. If you stumble then do same thing—move on. Yes, just move on!

Sizzle and Salsa on Social Media

Selling and increasing employee engagement have been showcased by the stories of Bugsay White Water Rafting and Honoring Heritage of the Lopez Group of Companies. Let us now delve deeper into the principles and practices of amplifying brands and priming up profits with the application of powerful storytelling to market to a much larger audience over the internet.

The traditional way was to call in an advertising agency when sales dropped or needed boosting. The advertising agency executives would look at the challenge, prepare a newspaper or billboard mockup ad, write a jingle about the features and advantages of the product, or shoot a 60-

second video of a pretty girl flashing her shiny white teeth while using THE "magical" product. They will then blast the jingle on the airwaves, put up a large billboard on the highway, and then pray for profits to pump up. This is what actor-comedian turned professor John Cleese claimed does not work but is still being done by advertising and media companies to prolong the life of the advertising industry.

Today, less and less people pick up a newspaper or a glossy magazine. Fewer and fewer people listen to a commercial radio station. People today curl up on their sofas and beds with a tablet or a laptop instead of watching any program on television. Our choices of entertainment and education have become focused and individualized. A cloud called the internet and social media has engulfed our lives and has made a big impact on the way we make our choices and our purchases. Our potential customer at the open end of our sales funnel is exposed to a near- infinite amount of options and invitations from thousands of sellers and businesses trying to push their products and services. It is mayhem in the marketplace.

Yet, the same technology that has blasted the globe wide open can be harnessed to catch the tiger by the tail and tame it. Today, we have to bring our story to the marketplace through the internet and social media and we have to tell it more creatively. Yes, a good story is a good start, but its packaging and posting is also extremely important today. In the past, business storytellers have claimed that content is king. Now they qualify that yes, content may be king but it is the delivery, the posting that is queen and she wears pants that need to be decked with roses, rainbows, and rhythm.

Here are factors we need to remember and consider before we get on the social media soapbox and pitch away our stories.

- We need an audience, and that audience is spread far and wide. It is invisible and is constantly on the move. It is nebulous.

- We need to thus, precisely define our customers and know their age, gender, educational levels, attitudes, beliefs, resources, free time, accessibility, likes and dislikes, preferred language, and decision-making process. If we model our target customer incorrectly, then we end up barking up the wrong tree in cyber space. Our marketing plans will fail and our bottom lines will rapidly go into the red.

- We need to recognize that our potential customer is now faster and sharper, is learning rapidly, and is being wooed by scores of others who want to tell their own story.

- We need to be razor-sharp when choosing the time to tell and share our story. Good timing is not just important, it is crucial. In early 2014 when Malaysian Airlines Flight 370 disappeared over the South China Sea, their marketing campaigns continued to run on the internet. Imagine people caught up in the unfortunate news and at the same time being exposed to promotions by the involved airline. This added fuel to the sad fire that was burning over the news wires.

- Finally, what is most volatile about our audience and potential customer is she has the power to cause a change in the plot, the theme, the flow, and the message of our story with just a few quick clicks on her laptop.

This last factor is a valid concern today for the same reason it presented a valid concern when the Lopez Group started their employee engagement campaign. The group was then worried about the lightning-fast, messenger bird called Twitter.

These are the advantages of serving our stories with a sizzle and a salsa over social media:

- It is easy to define our target customer because social media captures all data. Thus, age, gender, preferences, profession, and geographical location can all be determined.

- Even on a constantly spinning world, our voice and posts can be shared at the exact time and day of the week when the target customer is most receptive to tuning in to our story.

- More than just being able to zero in on our audience and our customer in the targeted geographical location, we are, in addition, also able to catch his attention over his preferred channel on social media. We can reach him through blogs, podcasts, video-logs, images, and even through elite conversations on, say, LinkedIn.

- In traditional face-to-face storytelling, professional storytellers are highly skilled at reading, assessing, and measuring signs of their audience's level of interest,

- engagement, and excitement. This is also possible on social media. Interest, engagement, and even action taken can be measured and logged through click-ins, click-throughs, shares, re-tweets, and eventual buy-ins.

Face-to-face storytellers are flexible, intuitive, and organic. They get their energy from audience interaction and they mix and match their histrionics to serve their audiences better. Professional marketers, digital story tellers on the internet and social media, can do the same with gigantic impact and real-time results.

Storytelling on Social Media is complex but doable; it costs little but has a huge impact on profits.

A Story: Ramadan 2014 and World Cup Football

Coke sales were not exactly falling, but they recognized a great combination of events coming together in Indonesia from the upcoming Ramadan season, the World Cup Football series, and a new, incoming, popular president. They decided to ride that nation's wave of popularity, so early in the year, Coke and its creative partners got together and decided to churn up multiple, people-oriented stories on the airwaves with the three events in mind. They came up with a plan to segment the story creation in three stages:

- Stage One, Inspire: Ask their target market what their wishes were for Ramadan season. Most responded with, "I want to go home, get out of the metropolis to spend time with family."

  This question was raised and diffused through traditional media like moving billboards, television commercials, and talk shows, etc. The responses from their audience also began to pile up on social media channels.

- Stage Two, Engage: Social media marketers got onboard and fueled the conversations and posts over multiple social media channels and then backed them up with video logs plus offers of free drinks, etc. At 6 weeks from launch date, the campaign began to pick up speed. Thousands of positive reviews, responses, shared posts, and re-tweets began to flourish.

- Stage Three, Celebrate: Right in the midst of the religious holiday season, stories of family reunions and happy, emotional encounters in the form of pictures, videos, blogs etc., ruled the airwaves. By the 10th week after its launch, the campaign had surpassed its projected objectives and targets, and Coke continues to be "the real thing" for Indonesians.

How did they do it?

- They defined their audience: millennials between the ages of 13-30, football lovers with a penchant for brands.

- They timed it right: launched six weeks before Ramadan and ran all the formats in tandem with the time slots when their target would be watching the World Cup series.

- They placed it right: geographical locations—outside the metropolis, in the malls, around universities, and wherever young sports fans hang out to watch and talk football.

- They also looped in their mothers in the Inspire stage and the Celebrate stage to reinforce the emotional bonds and to drive in the values of family and faith

- They spoke the truth, simply. In all their media campaigns, the language used was relevant and popular. They kept their promise of bringing together families and celebrating success.

It goes without saying they also measured their performance correctly and put in the right amount of dedicated effort to support the story and keep it moving on.

And yes, the job of a storyteller—whether to sell, to entertain, or to inspire—never ends. Every season and every day, just like every other 7-year old, our audiences and our market constantly need new stories to be created out of thin, thin air.

7 Leading, Happily Ever After

Leadership, they say, is a moment of insight. It is a journey towards a distant vision—a symphony of thoughts, words and action.

People do not get stirred by inanimate data. People are moved by ideas, emotions, and insights. It is the uniqueness of fresh perspectives that affects the hearts and minds of people. From such internal sightings or in-sightings, the possibility of a better life arises. These future possibilities are vivid images rich in emotions of hope and desire. They are called visions.

Conceived in a leader's mind, these images and emotions spread like wildfire, lighting up the minds and warming the hearts of many people. Fueling up such a beautiful symphony is done through stories—stories of possibilities and stories of inspiration.

Stories a Leader always carries

Every one of us needs to recognize the impact of putting across transformational truths through the HeART of Story. Following are the three genres of stories that every leader should always keep handy to authentically connect, engage, and influence one's world.

A story of humor and happiness:

Humor works best when you, the leader-storyteller, are the clown, bungler, or fall guy in a situation and when you tell a story about yourself from the third person perspective. You can start with, "I know of a small town hick who once.....and so on." This story will come in handy to build rapid rapport. It will make you appear down to earth and will endear yourself to both familiar and unfamiliar audiences. Humor targeted at oneself is an exercise in humility and it is the shortest distance between two hearts.

A Story: I Thought I was Famous

The heat was unbearable in the Hyundai Innovation Lab within the Gawad Kalinga Enchanted Farm at Angat, Bulacan, Philippines. The event was the 2014 Social Business Summit attended by social innovators and social enterprises. The topic was health and wellness.

Large industrial fans blew air but the wind wasn't having any cooling effect. People were sitting up on the chairs but it seemed they were staying on the chairs out of courtesy and in consideration of the fact that this was an event they chose to attend. The previous speakers were interesting, but none of them made the audience forget the sweltering heat. And then, Benjamin O. Yap, chief operating officer of United Laboratories Inc. (Unilab), stepped behind the podium.

"So, guess what?" he began. "This Enchanted Farm is a long ways from civilization and I suppose the cooling comforts of civilization have a hard time reaching this far. I, personally, had to spend for a chopper ride to get here. Well, it was fun and it took less than 15 minutes to get here. The interesting part was when we landed on the open lot near one of the settlements, scores of little children swarmed up to the helicopter. As I stepped out, all of them came up to me and began to take my hand to respectfully touch it to their foreheads, saying '*Mano po*!"

"I hadn't realized how well known and famous I was in these parts of the woods! I loved the adulation and I began to shake hands and nod, and pat their heads, and smile and wave. I couldn't help it! There were so many and this felt good. I felt important, well-known like a celebrity. After 20 minutes of nodding, patting, and waving I began to walk away from the children. That's when several of them, in unison, asked me, "Sir, who are you and what is your name?"

At this, the audience burst out laughing and the kindly speaker, Benjamin O. Yap then transitions into telling the audience about how 12 million more such children will be born in the Philippines within the next 10 years. He spoke of how the first 1,000 days of their lives will be crucial to their physical, mental, and spiritual wellbeing.

In the next 30 minutes he continued to expound upon the subject of safe birth and safe development in the first 1000 days of a child. All through those 30 minutes, the industrial fans continued blowing ineffectively, drops of sweat kept on gathering on listeners' brows, yet they sat there, eagerly hanging on his every word.

A story that educates:

Think back to a time when you went "Aha!" over a new subject matter at work or in life. It could have been an innovative process or a new philosophy in relating with others. Talk about how it took you a while to understand and accept. Describe how the blocks eventually fell away in places and you saw a fresh image, a novel construction. Share this story and make it relevant to the challenges your team may be having in accepting and adapting to change. If you choose to make yourself the hero, make sure you are a humble hero, not haughty or smug.

A story that inspires:

Recall a time when the kindness, compassion, or struggles of another person touched your life. Explain how it left you stronger, braver, and more driven towards your mission and purpose in life. Among the many possible applications of stories and storytelling, this application takes credence over all. The reason is mentioned in the first three chapters of this book. It is because stories reach into the deepest parts of the human mind to touch hearts, create drive, and propel movement.

These handy genres of stories have impact. They are priceless and timeless in leading self and others.

Storytelling Legacies of Leaders

In the mid-1930s India, a spritely old man wrapped up in loincloth spoke of freedom, compassion, and peace. Mahatma Gandhi carried a big stick, marched across the nation to pick up a fistful of salt by the ocean, and eventually liberated the country. He spoke to his people through painted visions and he touched hearts through parables of possibilities, "Change," he said "must come from the inside. We must become that change."

A few decades later in America, another visionary stepped on the podium and shortly after, set aside the text of his prepared remarks to improvise. Addressing a crowd of many thousands, he declared his dream—people from all corners of the country, from all walks of life, children of all races living together as one "to turn the jangling discords of our nation into a beautiful symphony of brotherhood." He announced his vision to the world to change a nation.

In the early 1980s in the Philippines, a journalist-turned-statesman chose to stand up against tyranny. Amid the toughest of odds, he flew home, stepped off the plane, and walked into the waiting jaws of death. This act of courage gave life to a story that inspired millions to act. Fired by his example and call of, "The Filipino is worth dying for!" the first ever people power revolution produced a peaceful transfer of leadership and changed the country's future. People power became a global model for bringing about change at the country level.

In comparison to the last 20 years, the rate of progress and the proliferation of information and technology have been exponential and show no signs of plateauing. How people will regulate and sustain life stories in the future is unimaginable. The stories of today are flourished in diverse formats. They are told and retold to sound and music, in dance, in art, in words, in moving images, all in bytes and pixels. Stories travel, morph and multiply at the speed of light with a cursory glance and the touch of a fingertip.

Will this explosion of knowledge and ideas through technology ever change the concept and the heart of telling stories? The answer is a flat out no!

Here's why:

- Wherever they may sit, leaders enhance their credibility and authenticity through storytelling to spark the change they seek. Storytelling does much, merely by advocating and counter-advocating propositional debate, which leads to increased discussions.

- Storytelling is focused on the future. It is not just an extrapolation of the present. It swirls emergent, new phenomena and nourishes it by downplaying the doubts and misconceptions of yesterday.

- Stories are about human empowerment and real transformations in organizations. Stories are about humanity. Stories are about us transforming into a better us. Stories are about us wanting to know who we are and about us wanting to reach for the stars.

A story is like mist that develops on the outside, but the wisdom emerges from the inside. When a story touches our hearts, it takes hold of us forever and silently sets us free. This is a never ending journey. It is also a never ending symphony. As long as this quest exists, stories will always fuel and fire us. And, since this is a never ending quest, we will always be leading ourselves and others happily into the ever after through stories.

That is the HeART of stories

A Story: Big B as a Brand

"Wherever I stand, all queues begin from there."

"It is not just difficult to catch a criminal like me, it is impossible."

"Ooph, your principles and your ideals, what use are these principles? You cannot grind together all your ideals and serve yourself two square meals!"

Quips like these from his movies in the late 70s and 80s earned him the moniker of the Star of the Millennium in India and abroad. He was the tall, dark, towering inferno that blazed across Indian cinemas from the mid-70s to the-90s.

When he reached his 50s, his star slowly began to fade. He chose to go on a sabbatical of silence for a few years and then came back looking refreshed, rejuvenated and wearing a distinguished looking silver-haired goatee. He re-entered the movie industry quietly playing elderly roles and then, again, for the last two decade has again become the toast of tinsel town India.

As a young actor he knew the power of a story and storytelling on the big screen. He knew emotions, angst, and the power of action in good storytelling. As a mature and bearded actor and businessman, he also learned the power of brand storytelling. He began rehashing lines from his old movies, created skits, and taught himself how to host a television show. He now sustains his personal brand, called Big-B, through social media.

A few years back, Coolbrands a company that studies and publishes stories of the best brands in the world interviewed him. Here is the essence of how he continues to further define himself, "my fans have always stayed by my side. Through Twitter and Facebook, I interact and answer every comment or message. I call them my Extended Family."

Now in his seventies, Amitabh Bachchan is still the biggest name in Indian Cinema. He sustains his own brand by allowing the over 50 million members of his extended family to continue telling his story.

A Story: Macintosh the Hero of 1984

"In 1958, a technology named Xenography was created but the Big Blue ignored it.

In 1968, a company called DEC invented the mini-computer but the Big Blue snubbed its existence and importance.

In 1977, another company put together Apple II but the Big Blue claimed it is too small to be of any worth to businesses.

At the turn of the next decade, the Big Blue wanted total control of the personal computer market. It wanted world domination, claimed a young man in a double-breasted suit and a bow-tie on January 24, 1984. It was at that time that he unveiled a protagonist, a hero called Macintosh to a screaming mass of 2,000 onlookers. This protagonist, Macintosh, then addressed the crowd. His first heroic and digital words were, "Hello, I am Macintosh. It sure is great to get out of that bag. Unaccustomed as I am to public speaking, I'd like to share with you a maxim I thought of the first time I met an IBM mainframe: Never trust a computer you can't lift. Obviously, I can talk right now, but I'd like to sit back and listen. So, it is with considerable pride that I introduce a man who has been like a father to me: Steve Jobs."

Those were the days of no PowerPoint, no Keynote, and no Prezi. In short, there were no colorful audiovisuals. But Steve Jobs, speaking in an intimate, dramatic storyteller's voice, changed the world by making the Macintosh the hero of his story. Today, years after his death, he continues to inspire the world not just with the brilliant products launched by his company, Apple, but with the memories of his legendary ability to lead through the art of storytelling.

Notice how another one of Steve Job's famous quotes can be compared to storytelling.

"… you can't connect the dots looking forward; you can only connect them looking backwards. So you have to trust that the dots will somehow connect in your future. You have to trust in something — your gut, destiny, life, karma, whatever."

Good storytelling depends a lot on gut feelings, gut reactions, linking, joining, adding, big-picture thinking, and moving forward on trust and tactile intelligence.

A Story: A Country in Jail

After spending nearly three decades in jail, a tall gaunt man steps out and announces to the world, "I was talking to another inmate in prison and he claimed unhappiness at having been unjustly locked in. At that moment, I had this amazing realization that it wasn't I who was jailed for almost 30 years but it was my country, my nation that had been in chains much, much longer. This was the truth and it is my mission to free my country."

Every single day thereafter, until his death, Nelson "Madiba" Mandela travelled the world telling them the story of suffering, of sorrow, and of racial injustice until the world responded to the plight of 50 million South Africans.

He then went on to become that country's president and to win the Nobel Peace Prize. He remains a shining example of human rights activism. During the last few decades of his life, as South Africans worked to heal and build their nation, Mandela's mission became that of national storyteller. He did not just talk the promoter's talk. He lived his talk, upholding the vision of everything that South Africa hoped to be. Without him weaving in the right values through repeated storytelling, his countrymen might not have gotten to know and love their nation as they do now.

These are powerful stories of influential leaders in their own fields and their ability to employ and leverage the power of authentic and heartfelt stories. Each of them promoted a different core Truth and exercised a unique style through various media, but every single one of them is a raconteur in his own right.

At this stage, let me leave you with a last story for this book, the HeART of STORY

A Story: Commitment to a Craft

The event was only just weeks away and I was very excited. I'd paid my registration fee and I decided I'd take the day off from family, friends, and other social commitments. The day of the event was on a Saturday so I didn't have to worry about school. I was eager to polish my English Grammar. As an elementary school teacher in the Philippines, I was not as concerned about my spoken English as I was about my written English. I needed to get a good handle on that angle because I wanted to be a better teacher in the future for my kids.

Early that Saturday, I arrived at the venue of the seminar. Nearly two hundred other teachers, principals, and administrators of different schools were already there. We all registered, had our snacks, and excitedly settled down in the large, covered, but non-airconditioned hall. There was a humongous buzz and chatter in the room. Nevertheless, from where I was, close to the stage, I didn't mind the noise.

A few minutes later, an elderly lady who appeared to be the organizer, came on stage and made an announcement. "I am sorry to tell you but there has been a slight change in the program. We were supposed to have a seminar on English Grammar Skills but the speaker called in sick last night and in her stead, we've brought in another speaker, who will talk to us about Communicative Leadership. I hope that'll be okay?" she said.

A mumbled grumble and a few raised voices went across the room, but courtesy and kindness being our culture, most smiled and settled down to what may come. The speaker, who was introduced and then stepped on stage, was a young-looking man with salt-and-pepper hair. He smiled and apologized, saying he was sorry that he couldn't do English Grammar Skills but that he'd share some really good and useful things about Communication and Leaderships Skills.

I was initially disappointed, but the guy was funny and open, so I settled into my chair and took my paper and pen out. A few minutes into the seminar, I had begun—like many others—to lean forward, laugh, nod, smile and respond to the speaker and his interactive exercises and stories about leadership. This is good, I said to myself. As I looked around, I felt others were happy and participative in their seats too.

But at one of the last tables, there were a bunch of elderly people from our profession who were out of sync with the whole class. They were talking more loudly than normal. A couple of them picked up and chatted loudly on their mobile phones, even as most of the teachers around naturally knew this to be impolite. It wasn't very nice, how they were behaving, I thought. I looked back at the speaker and I realized that he too was conscious of this little group. He made several attempts to involve them in the general discussions and the activities. He even walked up close to them and tried to make them smile, but it seemed like this little group had made up their mind to disrupt the proceedings. I realized that the whole group in that open-air hall had sensed the deliberate disruption. It was, I must tell you, a little embarrassing, us being teachers and all.

Come the morning snack break, the speaker unplugged himself from the microphone on his collar and politely walked up to their table. I stood up and followed expecting a showdown like the one at OK Corral. When I was within earshot of the group I heard this.

Speaker:	Hi! Good morning people! Is everything okay here?
Group Spokesperson:	Yes. All okay.
Speaker:	I did notice that many of you have been busy on your own here.
Group Spokesperson:	Yep, that's true.
Speaker:	Are the proceedings of the day okay for you? Is there anything I can do to help?
Group Spokesperson:	Well, now that you bring it up, we are not happy.
Speaker:	Not happy with me? My subject?
Group Spokesperson:	Not really. We are upset at the organizer who promised us one thing but is delivering us another.
Speaker:	Oh, that one! Correct me if I am wrong but wasn't that cleared already this morning?

Group Spokesperson:	Yes, but we are still upset and unhappy for being short-changed.
Speaker:	I am sorry and I do understand but this is out of my hands. May I just call back the organizer to take this up with you?

Saying this, he hailed the organizer to their table and gently moved back a few steps. He then leaned against a wall and stood there. Meanwhile, the conversations at that last table got a bit rough and a lot of bickering began to take place back and forth. I stayed and listened for a while and so did others. The bickering continued and scores of people from the rest of the crowd began to step out for lunch, for a drink or a cigarette.

Sill a bit concerned, I stepped out, had a quick lunch, and headed right back into the room. A day that I'd looked forward to for so many days was turning out to be ugly. I was mad and ashamed of being a teacher all at the same time. When I got back to the room the scene at the disruptive table hadn't changed. I looked at the wall where the speaker had slid away and was aghast to see that he hadn't moved an inch from his position. He was standing exactly the way he was standing before I'd stepped out for lunch. His hands were pressed behind him against the wall and he was leaning on his palms, with the sole of his left foot on the wall. He didn't look upset, hungry or tired. It just seemed as if he was hoping the battle at the table would go away.

I sat down and began to chat with people at my table. Every now and then, we glanced in the direction of the disruptive group and the speaker. Nothing changed. There was nothing we could do. We were all young and we were pretty junior in this profession and industry. Another hour and a half went by. The scene across at the OK Corral was still the same. Some participants began to leave. Others walked up to the doors and windows and lit up cigarettes. I felt sad. We are a kind and courteous people and this scenario just didn't fit into our culture and values.

After nearly 3 hours of standing against the wall, I saw the speaker move and walk up to the table. At first he just went and stood there quietly and erect. There seemed to be an expression of mercy and disappointment in his eyes at the same. The smokers at the doors and windows moved to within earshot of the table. Others outside also stole back into the room. Those sitting at the nearby tables sat alert but pretended not to be paying attention. And then he spoke to members of the disruptive table.

Speaker:	Is it okay if I ask you all a few questions?
Group Spokesperson:	Okay.

Speaker: Is it correct that you planned to spend this day here in this hall today?

Group Spokesperson: Aha, yep!

Speaker: Is it correct that you set aside all your other commitments to be here all day?

Group Spokesperson: Yes.

Speaker: Is it also true that you registered and made some financial investments for this event some weeks ago?

Group Spokesperson: Yes, of course!

Speaker: Would you say that all morning before the break, all the others and maybe you too picked up a few good pointers about Communication and Leadership?

Group Spokesperson: Yes, but that's not what we came here for.

Speaker:	That is correct and I respect that. Would I be right in saying that if all of you chose not to stay and to leave this hall this morning, you would not get your time, money and, more than all that, your hopes and expectations refunded. Correct?
Group Spokesperson:	Hmm, we see your point.
Speaker:	Then, in that case, may I request you please to let me put my microphone back on and create some value in learning for all of us in the hours that still remain useful in the day? If what I say and do doesn't create value then I, not the organizer, will refund your money. Is that okay?

This conversation was heard by most of those present in that room. The organizer had slowly slipped away somewhere and those at that table grunted their acceptance. The speaker returned to the front of the room and continued working through the remaining hours. The room slowly came back to life but the dark clouds of incident earlier hang in the hall like death.

The speaker continued to work professionally and quietly. He did put across a lot of value, not so much by the words he was putting together but by his behavior, and most of all, by how he'd handled the situation.

As the day came to an end, I slowly and steadily became proud of the fact that I'd chosen teaching as my profession. My family and friends used to tell me how thankless a profession it can be but that day, I felt it in my bones. I thought to myself, "*This is my life. This profession is my life's purpose.*"

At around 5 PM, I heard the speaker say these words, "To a leader it matters less how others treat and regard him. More important than that is how he responds to and regards others." With that, he smiled, thanked everyone, and brought the seminar to an end

People began to get up and slowly move towards the exit. Some applauded gently, while others stole a glance at the speaker and whispered their thank you. The people at that last table sat firm and glared at the rest of the crowd as they walked out. My heart was pounding hard and felt like popping out of my chest. I had to do something!

I gathered my stuff from the table, straightened my shoulders, and walked tall and straight towards the speaker.

I stood in front of him in plain view of everyone. When he looked up with moist eyes at me, I said to him in a voice loud enough for all to hear. "I have been touched and inspired by everything you have said and done here today. I have never witnessed so much patience, dedication, and commitment to a craft. Because of what I have learned, I too will remain committed to my craft and always remain a teacher." He looked at me with tender, smiling eyes with maybe just a sliver of doubt. I gently added, "In this Story of today, I have picked up a little Truth about life and living, *Maraming salamat po!*"

Same Story: Commitment to a Craft

Decades ago, I filled in for a speaker for some reason couldn't make it for her one-day training assignment. Her audiences were 200 school teachers and administrators. This was in the provinces of Philippines and her subject was English Grammar but the organizer said it'd be okay if I spoke about Communicative Leadership.

Eager to do a good job, I reached the venue 60 minutes everyone else and set up my speaker tools. As the crowds came in and settled down, I was announced as the speaker who'd replace the assigned speaker and my topic was also announced. The crowds sighed but let me happily begin my work.

We laughed, we played and we churned up the learning. Everyone participated excitedly except for a small group on a single table at the far end of the town hall. I tried to involve them in many creative ways but they seemed to be way too happy at doing their own thing and disrupting the whole class.

Come lunch break I unplugged the microphone from my collar and walked up to them.

"Everything okay here, folks?" I asked.

"No, not really!" bellowed the burliest of them all.

"Tell me about it, please," I added smilingly.

"Well you see we came in to pick up some grammar lesson from our favorite speaker and instead we get you and your high falutin topic."

"Oh, I am sorry, I mean no harm but I understand you even as I remember that the change was announced and clarified by the organizer."

"Yes, we know but we are not happy."

"Uh, okay, not in my hands to do anything but let me call the organizer and she'll sort out things for you."

So I let them talk. And, boy did they talk! They began arguing right after lunch at noon and didn't stop going back and forth over the same issue way until the mid-afternoon break. All through their quarreling I'd walked up to the side of room and with head hung low in shame leaned in and almost died into the wall. All others, nearly 200 of them, in the room began to sneak away and out for a coffee or a cigarette. Some stole side-eyed glances at me and I could sense them sizing up and feeling sorry for my embarrassment. I didn't move, I didn't flinch and all emotional turmoil within me showed no signs on my physicality. This profession was my passion and I knew that it required payoffs and sometimes these payoffs were hugely painful.

Come tea break I could make out from the sounds that peace hadn't settled in between the organizer and the burly group. I left my wall and very slowly walked up to their table and stood there quietly. It took them a few minutes but the buzz amongst them died down and they all had their eyes on me.

"Is it okay if I ask you all a few questions?" I asked.

"Okay?" replied the burly one.

"Is it correct that you planned to spend this day here in this hall today?"

"Aha, yep!"

"Is it correct that you set aside all your other commitments to be here all day?"

"Yes!"

"Is it also true that you registered and made some financial investments for this event some weeks ago?"

"Yes, of course!"

"Would you say that all morning before the break, all the others and maybe you too picked up a few good pointers about Communication and Leadership?"

"Yes, but that's not what we came here for!"

"That is correct and I respect that. Would I be right in saying that if all of you chose not to stay and to leave this hall this morning, you would not get your time, money and, more than all that, your hopes and expectations refunded. Correct?"

"Hmm, we see your point," growled Burly.

I continued in the same easy tome "Then, in that case, may I request you please to let me put my microphone back on and create some value in learning for all of us in the hours that still remain useful in the day? If what I say and do doesn't create value then I, not the organizer, will refund your money. Is that okay?"

They all grumbled but I head the burly one's eyes with eyes and he nodded approval. I am sure most everyone in the room heard the conversation and everyone's eyes were on Burly at that time. With extreme caution I dragged my feet away from them and with a prayer in my heart plugged the microphone back on my collar and began to work.

Usually, in circumstances like this something inside of us changes and becomes pure and powerful. Come 5:00PM, I had wrapped up my work very carefully and with a deep focus on adding value and doing something meaningful for these people. They were all teachers and teachers in my belief system are the noblest of us all. I must confess the energy in the room wasn't the same as it had been before lunch and yet this was something I loved to do and I let the love pour out.

As they began to leave the halls, some smiled and murmured a polite thank you. I was hoping someone would come talk me and say something about my work. That to us speakers and trainers is good fodder. It feeds our souls. But it seemed to day I wasn't going to get any until I looked up and there was a young woman right in front of me looking into my eyes. I managed a smile and she said, "I have been touched and inspired by everything you have said and done here today. I have never witnessed so much patience, dedication, and commitment to a craft. Because of what I have learned, I too will remain committed to my craft and always remain a teacher."

My knees almost buckled and I had to hold back my tears to smile at her when she added, "In this Story of today, I have picked up a little Truth about life and living, *Maraming salamat po!*"

Had my knees not turned soft at that time, I would have jumped up in the air and clicked my heels. I didn't at that time but every time I remember that moment my heart does leap with joy.

As this book comes to an end, I'd like to bring forth three questions that were often raised by pre-readers of the book and those that I had conversations with about stories and storytelling for leadership.

The three questions were:

1. Must the leader-storyteller always make himself the hero, the protagonist of the story and how?
2. Should the leader-storyteller share and tell more stories from the past, or of more of visions of the future?
3. How does the leader-storyteller know what qualifies any story the best story to tell in a given situation?

A leader-storyteller doesn't always have to make herself the protagonist of the story. She can conjure up fictional characters and incidents to put across a point or state a truth, taking care and making sure that the yarn she spins doesn't become too flimsy or synthetic. She can also use other people and tell stories of their sojourns and successes.

Here, she does have to make sure that she adds life and vibrancy to their emotions and experiences.

Now, if and when she does tell or write herself in as the protagonist then she has ease back from brow-beating and glorifying her own skills and capabilities as a hero. If she doesn't then it comes across as egoistical talk and creates a rift between the audience and herself. Our audiences, our clients give us their trust and faith only when they sense and are assured that the leader is not self-focused and is focused on their welfare and a greater good.

As a leader when we are using ourselves as the protagonist then our character plays out best when it is humble, ordinary in ways, transparent and achieves breakthrough results through reflection, self-correction and living up to the values she espouses.

The second question whether to use more stories from our pasts or create more visions can be best explained by defining and describing a concept called "creative tension." Creative tension comes about when the gap between our current reality and our visions of an ideal reality becomes unbearable and the stretch works like magnetic pull drawing us, making us work towards struggling towards the ideal—the vision.

Thus telling stories, both of the past and for the future is ideal. Stories from the past highlight our strengths, our faith in ourselves. Stories of the future draw and inspire us towards them. What percentage and proportion of each of the two kinds will depend on the organizational situation and the discretion of the leader-storyteller?

Lastly, about the question of what qualifies a story to be the best possible story, in a given situation, to drive change and inspire action.

The answer to that is quite straightforward. The best story to tell in a given situation by the leader-storyteller is that is the one that he is most afraid of telling or a story which excites and thrills him with visions of a scintillating tomorrow. Both these stories are powerful. One can unearth challenges and expose strengths and the second can charge and channel those strengths towards success and excellence.

Do take note that when I talk about stories people are most afraid to bring forth and tell, I do not mean a story that is distasteful and belittles others. It means a story which is loaded with a restless and an explosive truth about existing realities. It is a story that sets the leader and his community free from a physical, emotional or a spiritual bondage.

That is how to use stories and storytelling to connect with, engage and influence our worlds into a brighter tomorrow.

About Inner Sun

We at Inner Sun believe that every individual and every organization is a living system. At any given moment in this living system, there are three dimensions continuously at play.

The first is the dynamism that is innate, congenital, and embedded. In an individual, it is sometimes referred to as nature or personality; in a business organization, it may be referred to as "work culture".

The second dynamism is the one that exists outside of this system and is of many forms; the way that it is often referred to is the environment, economy, or ecology.

The third, the most vibrant, with a high potential to influence the inner and the outer dynamisms, is the dynamics of the process between the internal and external systems. The drivers of this intermediate dynamism are awareness, intelligence, emotion, memory, and action.

Inner Sun, the organization, focuses its own awareness, intelligence, and action towards this intermediary dynamism in all endeavors and interventions. The guiding elements behind our endeavors and interventions are:

- **Clarity** of thought, words, and action;
- **Creativity** of design, approach, and strategy; and,
- **Conscientiousness** of purpose and ultimate objectives.

Thinking free of bias and mental hammerlocks leads to higher clarity, creativity, and conscientiousness. As individuals and organizations strive for that status, their intelligences expand, interests broaden, and achievements soar.

We provide:

- Business solutions and interventions that bring about measurable results;
- Trainers who judge success not on their own performances but by how much the delegates learn;
- Personal service and tons of great value in an atmosphere of inspiration, support, and motivation;

About Raju Mandhyan

Author of five books, Cross-Cultural Leadership Coach and Learning Facilitator Raju Mandhyan has 15 years of experience in personal and organizational development. He has coached thousands of executives, delivered keynotes for hundreds of conferences across the Asian-Pacific region.

He is certified in Neuro Linguistic Programming, Mind Mapping, Appreciative Inquiry, American Management Association's Train the Trainer. He is also a Distinguished Toastmaster, Champion Speaker and the 2005-District Champion for Evaluations in the Philippines. In 2010, he had the rare honor of presenting at the American Society of Training and Development annual conference in Chicago.

Prior to his consulting career, Raju spent two years as an Engineer, two years as a Financial Consultant and 17 years as the CEO of an International Mercantile company handling projects for clients across the Mediterranean, Europe, Latin and North Americas. He has lived in India, USA and now lives with wife and three kids in the Philippines.

Look him up at www.mandhyan.com

other works

THE HEART OF PUBLIC SPEAKING

CREATIVE STARATEGIES AND TECHNIQUES FOR EFFECTIVE PUBLIC SPEAKING

Public Speaking is about ripping open your psyche and finding out what makes you worth anything, and it is about tearing down beliefs and then building new ones. This book provides you with creative strategies and techniques on how to choose the substance, build the structure and employ the style that'll help you effectively and delightfully add value to the lives of your audiences.

THE HEART OF HUMOR

TALES AND TECHNIQUES FOR A CREATIVELY FUNNIER YOU AT HOME AND AT WORK

Powerful and profound insights into what exactly humor is and backed by tales and techniques which, after practice, will make you a better observer of things, an acute and sensitive listener, a clearer and a faster thinker; an entertaining host and speaker and finally an all-around happy and wholesome person to be with.

THE HEART OF THE CLOSE

SUBTLE CLOSING STRATEGIES TO SOAR BEYOND YOUR SALES TARGETS

This book underscores a natural appreciation for the sales process. More than the "how-to's," real-life experience and wit weave throughout the book and how simplifies complex concepts. This amazingly insightful book comes at an opportune time, when the intricacies of selling in this milieu invite a more evolved appreciation for being human than a successful sales person.

"Those who do not have power over the story that dominates their lives — the power to retell it, rethink it, deconstruct it, joke about it, and change it as times change — truly are powerless, because they cannot think new thoughts."

Salman Rushdie, author